C000202174

Today Tomorrow

*To my family
and Lucina*

Today Tomorrow

Collected Poems 1933–2000

by

George Bruce

*Who reads the Book of the Sea
reads the Book of Life*

Edited by Lucina Prestige

Preface by Edwin Morgan

Polygon

© George Bruce, 2001

Polygon
An imprint of Edinburgh University Press Ltd
22 George Square, Edinburgh

Typeset in Horley Old Style
by Edderston Book Design, Peebles,
and printed and bound in Great Britain
by Creative Print & Design, Ebbw Vale, Wales

A CIP Record for this book is available from the British Library

ISBN 0 7486 6299 5 (paperback)

The right of George Bruce
to be identified as author of this
work has been asserted in accordance with
the Copyright, Designs and Patents Act 1988

The Publisher acknowledges subsidy from

THE SCOTTISH ARTS COUNCIL

towards the publication of this book

Contents

A MAN OF INCONSEQUENT BUILD AND OTHER POEMS 1944–1964

HOUSES AND OTHER POEMS

PERSPECTIVES: POEMS 1970–1986
PROLOGUE VISIONS

FROM THE SHORELINE

THE DESERT AND OTHER MORALITIES

FOLK

A NEW PERSPECTIVE

PURSUIT: POEMS 1986–1998

RETURN

FOLK

PURSUIT

CREATURES

TODAY TOMORROW: HAIKUS AND OTHER NEW POEMS

Biography

George Bruce was born in Fraserburgh (1909), seaport of north-east Scotland, he was educated at Fraserburgh Academy and studied literature at Aberdeen University, graduating in 1932. In 1934 he began teaching English Literature and History at Dundee High School and married Elizabeth Duncan in 1935. He published his first collection *Sea Talk* in 1944. In 1947 he published *Selected Poems* and moved to Aberdeen in the same year to take up a post as Producer with the BBC. In 1956 he was appointed BBC Features Producer with responsibility for Arts Programmes, this required a move to Edinburgh, where he still lives today. He retired from the BBC in 1970. During this time *Landscapes and Figures* (1967) and *Collected Poems* (1970) were published, and he continued to write theatre criticism and review books for *The Sunday Times* well after his retirement.

From 1971 to 1973 George Bruce was appointed first Fellow in Creative Writing at the University of Glasgow; during 1976–77 he was visiting Professor in the department of English Literature at the College of Wooster, Ohio, USA; there he was awarded an Honoury D.Litt. He lectured at Washington Lee University, and was visiting Professor at Prescott College, Arizona, USA (1974) and also visiting Professor at Union Theological Seminary, Richmond, Virginia, USA (1974). In 1982 he became Scottish Australia Creative Writing Fellow at the University of New England, New South Wales, Australia. During this period he continued writing and lecturing internationally. His own range of publications at this time included a monograph on *Anne Redpath* (1973); *Festival in the North* (1975), the story of the Edinburgh International Festival; *Some Practical Good* (1975), which was a history of The Cockburn Association and *William Soutar 1898–1943: the Man and Poet* (1978). In 1984 he was awarded an OBE.

His abiding concern has been writing poetry, and aside from being widely published in various literary magazines and journals, and broadcast on radio, he published two further poetry collections, *The Red Sky* (1985) published by St Andrews Press, North Carolina, USA and *Perspectives* (1987). His most recent publication, *Pursuit: Poems 1986–1998*, won the Saltire Scotsman Award for the best Scottish book of 1999. He was awarded an Honorary D.Litt from Aberdeen University in 2000. George Bruce is an honorary President of the Scottish Poetry Library and honorary member of PEN. Current work-in-progress includes a new collection of poetry, a book of Haikus and an art-poetry collaboration *The Sea Woman*, with the artist John Bellany.

Preface

'The child is father of the man,' wrote Wordsworth, but this can be a dangerous doctrine. In 'On the Shoreline', an essay written by George Bruce on his own childhood in and around Fraserburgh on the north-east coast of Scotland, he recalls a free and happy time in that environment. 'The running boy, the diving boy, the boy challenging the currents and cold of the North Sea was its product.' The physicality, the hardihood, the challenging of the cold encouraged him to transfer these qualities to the headlands of Buchan in the much anthologised poem 'Kinnaird Head', with which he became identified (like Yeats with 'The Lake Isle of Innisfree') in a way that was unfair to himself. Hard rock; hardy person. But one must move away from that, and he did. What the harsh fishing-town environment gave him was a fine eye and ear and nose for detail: 'thigh boots deep in squeaking herring', wind that 'twists the sycamore's branches', the sea with 'its fog in the nostrils of the boy', the 'red-eyed mackerel', the smell of the 'warm leathery hide' of the milkman's horse.

Giving voice to a local community, being 'a poet of the north-east', proved restrictive to a poet whose career turned out to be a long one, and he found himself, still with a natural boyish eagerness and enthusiasm, opening up new subjects and new styles, and sometimes revisiting early themes from a new perspective. He probes the reactions of an Australian Aborigine in a tax office; he re-records from television the shooting of a Laotian peasant; he writes an elegy for the Polish theatre director Tadeusz Kantor. His engagement with these subjects is characteristically unlanguid. You watch him watching. You fix him fixing. Not unexpectedly, he is attracted by the eye of the painter, pounces on Rembrandt and Velasquez, Cézanne and Bellany, follows with sympathetic insight the 'pursuit' each engages in as he goes after the uncapturable reality of a blue mountain or a woman cooking eggs, something beyond words, yet dragged back into words by a filament of poetry:

> the egg, the water in the glass,
> the gourd, the features of the old
> woman, the boy, the seller of water,
> water of life he sold – that
> crystalline freshness was his
> to sell, to sell that which was
> beyond price –

This seems a long way, both in its lyrical movement and in its theme, from the dour, thick-set certainties of 'Kinnaird Head'. And interestingly, 'Kinnaird Head' is itself the subject of a corrective comeback in 'Cliff Face Erosion', where the fact of geological change is acknowledged as a source of wonder, and if there is a human analogy it is an acceptence of ravages that are none the worse for not being immortal:

> *no more are you the bastion that you were,*
> *resisting and denying access to sea's force,*
> *the great wave falling from you, and you*
> *remained yourself. Now to the gnawing salt,*
> *the flux of waters, cross-fire of elements,*
> *you concede. Ravaged, penetrated, scuffed,*
> *deep-graven – your face is witness,*
> *as is the human face, to the years.*
> *I look upon your face and it is mine.*

The range and depth of these poems stand ready to surprise readers who may have underestimated a writer who went his own way and did not push his wares. Here he is now, collected for your enjoyment, with a deep and moving trawl of many years, from fisheries to happenings, from the seagull to the kookaburra, from huge impersonal scarred headlands to an agate being polished by the warm hands of his wife.

Edwin Morgan

Introduction

I began to write verses when I was seven years old – or so my Aunty Madge told me. No doubt this was like other children, but I persisted. This book begins with poems written in 1933, but it was not until the late 1930s that the thrust of my poetry – its subject and style – compelled me to write as I did, resulting in the publication of *Sea Talk* in 1944.

It seemed to me then, when the death of a deteriorating civilisation was imminent, to put one's trust in the continuity of values as expressed in the life of a small community was against all logic. Yet largely unconsciously, in my attachment to the sensitive, economic style in Ezra Pound's *Hugh Selwyn Mauberly*, and the poetry of William Carlos Williams, I was acquiring the appropriate style for realising the fact and the sense of the fact; this in the first instance being the idea of the endurance, courage, integrity and skills of the fisherman, and associated with this the cliff, steady in a welter of waters. These became symbols of permanence. From such a base, and the happiness of my upbringing in a loving family, followed by the happiest of marriages, my poems tended to become, less a commentary on society and more a celebration of life.

Years later in 1996 I was presented with a photograph which showed a cliff crumbling. I felt devastated. The symbol of permanence had gone. Yet this had to be accepted. I wrote *Cliff Face Erosion*. Edwin Morgan in his *Preface* recognised it as a key poem. From then I found a new freedom, and also a new recognition of what my poems must encompass. I could look on the waters of the sea, and there was a new beginning waiting to be written on the page

Who reads the Book of the Sea
reads the Book of Life.

Now I wrote on a wider canvas. From the celebration of the wholeness of the creation of the earth, which we share with its creatures, as in *The Fox and Lucina* to the Theatre of the Absurd in my tribute to Tadeusz Kantor. I must show in the imagination of poetry the disastrous effects on society of the misdealings of rulers and politicians. And after this book – who am I to tell?

George Bruce

Editor's Note

While assisting George Bruce with the preparation of his manuscript for *Pursuit: Poems 1986–1998* (published by Scottish Cultural Press) on 10 March 1999 – his ninetieth birthday – it occurred to me that ninety was the right age for a review of George Bruce's life of poetry – a long overdue collected work.

This book reveals the fascinating development of his poetry: from his earliest poems in 1933 through to the extraordinary achievement of his most recent writing, where he arrives at a new poetical dimension. His perceptive eye and youthful imagination are more in evidence than ever. This review of George Bruce's poetical journey should interest scholars and poetry lovers alike.

George Gunn sums up Bruce's lifetime of work perfectly, when he says (*Chapman 2000*):

> 'If Scotland's passage through the twentieth century has to be charted then we could do no better than to use the poems of George Bruce as a guide, for as he wrote of Velazquez . . .

> *He turned the searchlight of his mind*
> *upon each and every object equally,*
> *persons or things as if each in its*
> *difference, might through the precision*
> *of line and paint, each weighed in the*
> *balance of a mind, would yield*
> *final truth . . .*

Lucina Prestige

Bibliography

Sea Talk, Glasgow, Maclellan, 1944.
Selected Poems, Edinburgh, Saltire Modern Poets, 1947.
Landscapes and Figures, Preston, Akros, 1967.
The Collected Poems of George Bruce, Edinburgh University Press, 1970.
The Red Sky: Poems, The St Andrews Press, North Carolina, 1985.
Perspectives: Poems 1970–1986, Aberdeen University Press, 1987.
Pursuit: Poems 1986–1998, Edinburgh, Scottish Cultural Press, 1999

Acknowledgements

Poems in *Today Tomorrow, The Collected Poems of George Bruce, 1933–2000* have appeared in the following journals:
The Voice of Scotland (1937); *Contemporary Poetry* (USA); *The 40's*, published by Penguin; *Aberdeen University Review*, *Blackwood's Magazine*, *Lines Review*, *Akros*, *The Saltire Review*, *The New Saltire*, *Chapman*, *Interim* (USA), *Zed20* published by Akros, *The Aberdeen Press and Journal*, *The Scotsman*, *The Herald*, *Meanjin* (Australia), *NorthWords*, *New Writing Scotland*, *Scottish Book Collector*, *Cencrastus*, *The Magazine of the Architectural Heritage Society of Scotland*.

Other poems have appeared in the following books; *Poetry Scotland* (1943), *Modern Scottish Poetry*, *1920–1945* ed. Maurice Lindsay (1946) – and successive volumes; *A Book of Scottish Verse* (World's Classics); *Contemporary Scottish Verse: 1959–1969*; *A Very Still Life* (Atelier Books), *Poetry of the Forties* (Penguin); *The New British Poets* (USA); *The Oxford Book of Scottish Verse*; *A Scottish Childhood*; *Natural Light* published by Paul Harris; *The Five Touns Festival Collection*; *Where the Land meets the Sea*; *The Scottish Dog* (Aberdeen University Press); *Kapu a Tengerhez (A Gateway to the Sea)* – a bilingual anthology of Scottish Poetry, published by the British Council, Budapest (1998).

In Gratitude

I wish to record my gratitude to John Bellany for allowing me to reproduce his drawing of the *Sea Woman* for the cover of this book (see poem 'Sea Woman' p. 277). To Edwin Morgan for the preface. Also to Andrew Bruce and Jane Kellett for help in the preparation of the manuscript.

Today Tomorrow

The Collected Poems of George Bruce

1933–2000

Early Poems 1933

Early Poems 1935

The Changeless Metal

Only the contraries in the mind create
And hold together, holus bolus, that estate
Indivisible and incorporate,
That equates and generates
The robust sun,

Man and woman.

The sun holds his place
By that divine grace
Which states
One law of constancy,
All things begin and all things end,
The law which but exists in contrariety,
The Rose of forgetfulness
In rose of memory.

'All things are beaten into shape
All things begin and all things end'
– A schoolboy scratches on a slate.

The Young Man Dares Time

I will cheat Time
Said the young man
As only poet can
That builds in rhyme,

Or the painter
Who steals his light from nature
And hesitates in his stroke
Only that the glory
That from heaven broke
Now break from the mind's defecation
In mockery of Time and Time's generation.

Michael Angelo States the Impersonality of the Creation

The Time is neither nearer nor yet further off
For me to submit
Emblems of my draughtsmanship
For I am Time and my transcript
Creates the hour, makes articulate
What was inchoate, what before did not exist.

You are my statement
And represent
The Petrifaction
Of the universe

I traffic only in the fire
of generation and immolation.
You are but the feather in the wing
of the bird I teach to sing

Sea Talk
1939–1944

A Song for Scotland

A skull shoots sea-green grass from its sockets.
I saw it as the wave lengthened and flattened.
Moon whitened the cranium, plied its beams upon
The shooting sea-green hair.

You tell me not to stare
So in upon myself
Nor throw the arc-light
Of the mind.

But here my songs begin
Here their first thin irregular,
(Like the waver of the wind)
Yet sometimes taut, music.

The oar rots on the beach.
The skua breeds on the cliff.

A song for Scotland this,
For the people
Of the clearances,
For the dead tenements,
For the dead herring
On the living water.[1]
A song for Scotland this.

Inheritance

This which I write now
Was written years ago
Before my birth
In the features of my father.

It was stamped
In the rock formations
West of my hometown.
Not I write,

But, perhaps William Bruce,
Cooper.
Perhaps here his hand
Well articled in his trade.

Then though my words
Hit out
An ebullition from
City or flower,

There not my faith,
These the paint
Smeared upon
The inarticulate,

The salt-crusted sea-boot,
The red-eyed mackerel,
The plate shining with herring,
And many men,

Seamen and craftsmen and curers,
And behind them
The protest of hundreds of years,
The sea obstinate against the land.

My House

My house
Is granite
It fronts
North,

Where the Firth flows,
East the sea.
My room
holds the first

Blow from the North,
The first from East,
Salt upon
The pane.

In the dark
I, a child,
Did not know
The consuming night

And heard
The wind,
Unworried and
Warm – secure.

The Curtain

Half way up the stairs
Is the tall curtain.
We noticed it there
After the unfinished tale.

My father came home,
His clothes sea-wet,
His breath cold.
He said a boat had gone.

He held a lantern.
The mist moved in,
Rested on the stone step
And hung above the floor.

I remembered
The blue glint
Of the herring scales
Fixed in the mat,

And also a foolish crab
That held his own pincers fast.
We called him
Old Iron-clad.

I smelt again
The kippers cooked in oak ash.
That helped me to forget
The tall curtain.

A Boy's Saturday Night

In summer the sky
Was lit late.
Nearby the beach
Were stalls, swing boats,

Steam driven round-abouts
Gold horses of wood
Or bright red chair-o-planes
And mechanical music.

On the links stood
A boxing booth.
'Boys half price for the boxing.'
The fishermen spent money here.

Here Rob Burke was at work
Taking all comers
Till dark.
He put the finger of his glove

To his flat nose, snorted,
And then spat.
Short work was made of
Our Tom Scott.

We saw even the dust rise.
Outside the land was black.
'That's queer' I said,
'Sea's lit – like a lamp.'

Boys Among Rock Pools

Boys on knees, or prostrate, and scrambling
About rocks, by rock pools and inlets,
Noting with accurate eye the wash of water.
They hunt (O primitives!) for small fish,
Inches long only, and quicksilver,
But pink beneath the dorsal fin
Moving with superb locomotion.
Bodies bent, eyes all upon the prey –
Boys in shallow water with sun-warmed feet.

The Startled Hare

Hare leaps with eye of fear.
Sparse grass, sanded and salt, prompts.
And air – what daylight here! –
Through limb and limb cavorts.

Dust puffs at feet: he lollops free,
Where tern astride, or winging on, a minor breeze
Stares to the wind abundant sea.
This winter too before gorse breaks and beams.

At the Loch of Strathbeg

Space! – here runs astringent air
Across the loch fixed
In three miles of flat,
The habitat of thistle and hare.

Outpaced gull and tern
Swing in a catspaw's fuff.
By the shocked occasional tree
Wind twists to the fern.

Cower weasel in the wall,
Look upon our scenery.
The loch fixed
Tree torn from soil.

The Town

Between the flat land of the plain
And the brief rock – the town.
This morning the eye receives
(As if space had not intervened,
As if white light of extraordinary transparency
Had conveyed it silent and with smooth vigour)
The granite edge, edifice of stone –
The new tenement takes the sun.
The shop fronts stare,
The church spire signals heaven,
The blue-tarred streets divide and open sea-ward,
The air leaps like an animal.

Did once the sea engulf all here and then
At second thought withdraw to leave
A sea-washed town?

Kinnaird Head

I go North to cold, to home, to Kinnaird,
Fit monument for our time.

This is the outermost edge of Buchan.
Inland the sea birds range,
The tree's leaf has salt upon it,
The tree turns to the low stone wall.
And here a promontory rises towards Norway.
Irregular to the top of thin grey grass
Where the spindrift in storm lays its beads.
The water plugs in the cliff sides,
The gull cries from the clouds
This is the consummation of the plain.

O impregnable and very ancient rock,
Rejecting the violence of water,
Ignoring its accumulations and strategy,
You yield to history nothing.

For Hugh MacDiarmid

1. THE WINE TOWER

Now our poverty when most we need the Canon of a Giant Art,
That will contain disruption. What shape of life
Dare we to propagate in History? – An image
Holds the mind. A blind tower upon a basalt floor
Lips cliff, both subject to the force of air and sea.
This cube was the repository of wine for Frazer of Saltoun.
Fine wine. One took it upon the tips of alert senses,
Savoured it on palate and by intellect. So *we* present at once
To the unbound future, the supple muscle and the exquisitely
                                                    receptive nerve.

2. TOWER AND CASTLE

Violence without, within legend. Years ago the empty barrels
Roistered doon the braes. The castle wis lit,
An' extra men were put to roll more wine from tower
To hoose that stood well back ahint the cliff.
They say that more matured than wine therein. The dark
Once prisoned the old man's daughter wha' wantit
The wrang man: an' ballad like, the pointed rock aneath.
Had her. Her songsters were the gulls.

3. THE CASTLE TURNED LIGHTHOUSE

The present occupant of the house attends a new plant,
Powerful machinery operating to project a beam of light
For ten miles. Ball-bearing, frictionless lamp –
What immeasurable skill upon a thing!
As if the subtleties of the brain were taken out
And we left only to be minders of the machine,
Admirers of our suicide.

A Land without Myth

This is the land without myth –
From the crown of this low hill
To the useful country receding East
To the rectangular towns we have built;
Coast towns, granite pavemented, with drinking troughs
For the animals, electric standards, kiosks,
Large gasometers and excellent sanitation.
Parks and tennis courts are at the disposal
Of the young, and at the sea, gaiety,
Almost a semi-circle of amusement
Extending invitations to all couples,
At least in summer – but not (as you know)
This year though the sunlight remains
Astride the promenade and pier.
This is the land without myth.

Then all was idleness, and wealth
Like sand, or so it seemed,
Spread in the uncles' cars upon the beach.
Have the bazaars closed down,
And for us between the sea and the land
No prizes? Waste.
This is the land without myth.

The crab scuttles on the sea floor,
Hook dangles, net opens to the tide,
The boat's keel is still or moves
With the greater water movement.
Between the thumb and the first finger
The weighted line.

Look inland beyond the roof tops, behind
The allotments and the tin sheds.
(This is the land without myth.)
The coulter is in the soil,
The thin crop is on the iron rock
The field glitters like a new coin.

Here are neither mountains nor dark valleys
Here the shadow's length is man, or the tree
That is his, or the house he has built.

Years back the stones were lifted from the fields,
The animals driven to their holes, the land drained,
Dug, planted, the ground pieced out.
The heather was beat. The crop grew
On the hill. The paths were trod.
The land was peopled and tilled.
This is the land without myth.

By the burn the children collect
Small blue butterflies. The poppies are theirs.
For them the sun stands at attention,
The road stretches out in its blueness,
Their feet clatter upon it.
This is a known land,
A land without myth.

Sea Talk

to a Buchan Fisherman

1. Night holds the past, the present is manifest in day,
    In day activity, but night shuts the door –
    And within the mind hints of your old powers,
    Recollections of your associate, the sea.

    Now this night in tribute I write you
    And have you, your boys, your wife in mind
    The better for not being there where you are.
    Too much business there with winch running,
    Pulleys slipping, hawsers, horses, men, lorries, herring;
    Besides, being a cranner[2] I must note the fish
    And see to the salt. But here
    I remember again your boys on the beach at sun-down,
    Their graips at sods of sand,
    Their hands' flash for bait,
    Behind – sandhills with grass,
    In front the sea, that sea that binds to it
    The cottage on the cliff top or on the shore,
    Invades the ears of the boy, enters his eyes, binds him
    And the crustacea – monsters of the sea pools.

Consider the spider crab.
From the rock, half rock itself, pinhead eyes project,
The mechanism of movement awkward, legs propelled
A settlement for parasite, for limpet;
Passionless stone in the world of motion.
The pounded shells, a broken razor,
Mussel, fan, speak as much life.
O dark-haired fisherman who know the tides
And proper prices for the catch,
Here is the image of your skull.
Who will tell upon the shingle beach
Which the shell splinter, which the particle of the skull
Long bleached by the flow and ebb?

The sea binds the village,
Its salt constricts the pasture behind,
Its gale fastens the bent grass before,
Its fog is in the nostrils of the boy.
Your iron ship, a novelty to sea's age,
Puts out. Sea gives tongue to greater
Fears, deeds, terrors, than you can tell.
It's articulate in the crab, the hermit, spider, partan.
These tell the knowledge in your bone,
Over these your boat slips
And down to these grope line and nets.
Here breed the initiates of life
In rock chambers and on the floor beneath tide,
Beneath sway and trouble, undisturbed.

2.   Of Balbec and Finistère Proust wrote –
The oldest bone in the earth's skeleton,
The land's end of France, Europe, of the Old World,
The ultimate encampment of fishermen
Who since the beginning faced
The everlasting kingdom of fog,
Of shadows of the night. Coast
Contemporaneous with the great geological phenomena,
Remote from human history as the constellations.
And here upon a promontory
At the foot of the cliffs of Death,
Not, as might have been expected,
The timid essay towards life,
Nor yet a bastion threatening the sea's force,

But, peculiar growth on these rocks,
The tender Gothic with a spire flowering;
Below it the blunt stone faced apostles,
And at the porch the Virgin:
Enveloping all – salt fog.

To defend life thus and so to grace it
What art! but you, my friend, know nothing of this,
Merely the fog, more often the east wind
That scours the sand from the shore,
Bequeathing it to the sheep pasture,
Whipping the dust from fields,
Disclosing the stone ribs of earth –
The frame that for ever presses back the roots of corn
In the shallow soil. This wind,
Driving over your roof,
Twists the sycamore's branches,
Till its dwarf fingers shoot west,
Outspread on bare country, lying wide.
Erect against the element
House and kirk and your flint face.

The kirk looks graceless, a block house
To defy the last snort of winter,
The house shouldering the sea,
Dark as your ship inside, the windows locked,
The curtains heavy as if suspecting light.
Both bar the element, shut, as your face is shut,
To the subtle invaders, to fortune the anarchist
To the spies of Spring, to the lecher in the blood.

3.   Your face burgeons before me out of night,
Blue jowled, nose aquiline, big mouth,
Fisher grey eyes with resolute and phlegmatic look.
Nor do these features tell all the sea story
And in imagination blossoms that angular, garrulous man
Who skippered *The Gem*, matching your ease
With his reckless tongue. His name was Gatt:
Lithe, restless, drunken, bigoted, but like you too
Accepting the thump and peril of water.
Both hammered between these – poles apart –
Water and the Word – both gifts of God.

Between these your feet are shaped, your hands helped
By water, pebble, cliff and sky.
Blue rocks nose above the sand about your feet,
Feet expert and attentive to the ship's swing.
Your hands like women's in their dexterity,

Never fumble needle or net, rope or wheel.
Their clutch is taught by the sea's clutch,
The small words of sea talk, the mumbling
And knocking at the little boat's side,
These pleasantries teach and the rest,
The unforgettable clap making even you merely awkward,
A doll only in a doll's house put together.

This is the gift of God.
Accept the road your feet have taken
Over the pebbles to the pier, from pier to deck boards.
You have seven paces on board, seven on return, no more,
Turning inward lest the sea have you.
Accept the sublit seas beneath – the squid,
The pink and purple prostrates, valvular jellies,
Fungoid jungle. Here globe, tube, cone, the final shapes
Have life, have mouths, erupt, move in currents
Without air and are still – lives crepuscular.
With these lands I have no acquaintance.
Accept them as you accept
The little fish leaping in the morning
From the net streaming into the scuppers.

Your life is strife,
Your nose has long snuffed wind harsh with salt,
You have seen plenty sour mornings,
But the day you took that shot to port – herring deck high –
Was fine, blowy and with sun. Cloud from the North
Piled up by the foremast and beat off fast South.
The gulls knew you were heavy loaded,
Met and escorted you,
Swinging just over you in the trough,
Just over you on the swell.
The boat's bow pressed on the water,
Under the stern the sea blackened,
The wave flattened out, but, resilient and very powerful,
Pushed at the strakes and hull.

The propeller forced water into spirals widening at the top,
Their track broadened behind,
Fell away, and mixed with expanse.
Did luck or judgement make that catch?
'Fifty mile oot aff Sumburgh Head' – the night airy
The moon behind fine cloud, some motion.

Certainty of hand despite the numbing night,
Sureness of feet despite the deck at odds with them,
Knowledge of course from compass and stars;
What conjunction brought success?
You know how sweet
To attribute success to the skill of eye and hands and feet,
How difficult
To walk with circumspection between pride and despair.

Do you not despair of the unspeculating eyes of fish,
Of the ignorance of oceans,
Of the infinite varieties of species
Articulating in their variety, indifference,
Creating to perish, perishing to create
The continuing indifferent sea face?

'Who hath measured the waters in the hollow of his hand
And meted out heaven with the span
And comprehended the dust of the earth in a measure
And weighed the mountain in the scales
And the hill in a balance?

Have ye not known? Have ye not heard?
Hath it not been told you from the beginning?
Have ye not understood from the foundations of the earth?'

Death Mask of a Fisherman

My dead father speaks to me
In a look he wore when dying.
The emaciated hands and limbs
Pass from the memory,
But that mask appropriate to that moment
When he balanced between two worlds
Remains to rise again and again
Like an unanswered question.

He was going very fast then
To be distributed amongst the things
And creatures of the ground and sea.
He was ready for the shells and worms,
(Outside the rain stormed
And the small boats at the pier jolted)
His eyes had passed to the other side
Of terror and pain.

Night had settled in each.
The dissipation of feature,
The manifestation of skull,
The lengthening of cheek,
The dark filtering into the hollows,
Told *one* thing:
What speed towards our mother!

But another image here too,
Something I had seen before
Caverned in the El Greco face,
Something presented to us
From the other side of dream;
Translatable only in hints from the breathless world.

Song for a Hero

There is no home for the hero.
Even when a boy he left his passions
At the pier. His eyes did not note them,
Nor the white handkerchiefs, but turned,
As the North controlled needle turns,
To the gulls who offered no memento.

Yet with the rest he had his curios,
The master key that opened all,
The starfish sporting one more limb,
The match-box with the double back,
Shells highly convoluted like a screw,
But these made exits from his heart.

And school was taken in his stride,
His gaze averted from it all,
Though capes and bays and distances
Were glanced at, recognised
As matters of potential interest.
Astronomy he was not taught.

Darkness ingathers the ship. The foam
Of many seas arches upon her bows.
The cargoes, corn for metal,
Make their change. And he takes stock,
Sees to delivery, hears the engine run,
And stands observant at the winch.

There is no home for the hero.
His head – like a head in profile,
The minted head on a coin –
Occupies the windy spaces
And holds predestined courses.

The Fisherman

As he comes from one of those small houses
Set within the curve of the low cliff
For a moment he pauses
Foot on step at the low lintel
Before fronting wind and sun.
He carries out from within something of the dark
Concealed by heavy curtain,
Or held within the ship under hatches.

Yet with what assurance
The compact body moves,
Head pressed to wind,
His being at an angle
As to anticipate the lurch of earth.

Who is he to contain night
And still walk stubborn
Holding the ground with light feet
And with a careless gait?
Perhaps a cataract of light floods,
Perhaps the apostolic flame.
Whatever it may be
The road takes him from us.
Now the pier is his, now the tide.

For Voyagers

The needle starts North.
There the still simplicity in the single gull
That hangs above the rock,
Or in the stone of the low wall, a shelter
For the wiry animals, or in stone
Of granite quarried in a treeless land
Or stone of basalt merely there
In the abrupt water, or stone
Of the hurled meteor, stone of planet.
Strange comfort, but comfort
To all men voyaging.

In Memory of a Submarine Officer

We remember him.
Especially his hope for a future,
As if he had private information
On Fate's next move,
Assurances the attack would cease
At least short of his breath.
The future would be there for him,
The tides, despite their treachery
Would recede, the clouds dissipate,
The world would resume.

We know his short legs stood him
At dials, power gauges, recorders of sorts,
Stood him ignoring seas, pustular rock life,
Expectant orifice of shark,
Porpoise swaddled in a welter,
And all the rest. Was he deaf
To every threat? – the great throb
Persuasive on the steel,
Accumulative as his touch
Directed machinery to deeper reach.

He stood – so we guessed –
Very securely, and cultivated
Dreams of his achievement
In drawing-rooms and on the radio,
Of his voice rising with assurance,
Of his meeting the great,
Of extraordinary happiness in store.
God cherish him his happiness
Such strength was in that dream
That Heaven budded there.

Epilogue

Hammered between – these poles apart,
Water and the Word – the Fisherman.
Here his life story, his dull windy morning,
His seasonal activity, his dealing,
Sleep, worship, his world.
He stands sure footed in what universe?

Beneath boards the weight of waters
Pressures, fluctuations, varying darknesses,
Degrees of light and subtle glooms.
Above – the customary skies
Of blessing and vicissitude.
His face is tanned and set
As is a compass.

What worlds of journeys his!

Between bigotry, the simple ecstasy
And order, discipline, he swings,
Yet seeing in all things easy, difficult,
Raw or superfine, the hand of God.

Between what worlds his range!

Motion at feet and hand and brain,
In this he stands, this his normality.
Poised, and for ever dangerous,
He holds his course.

Robin in the City

1. Hallo! you little sad messenger,
    Reminder of unalterable woes,
    Trespasser, your dress is inappropriate –
    A Spring bud red to blossom in snows.
    Here only are steel springs, the ayes and noes
    Of dry merchants with demand notes
    Short circuited by multiple stores.
    Go! Take your hints of country habitation
    Where the farm boy snores.

2. That sharp wisdom in your eyes
    Proclaims the hunger of centuries,
    Slips in upon even the remote heart
    Here held in city maladies.
    Your pertinent call reminds the too-cajoled mind
    That territories of Europe
    Frozen in their boundaries
    Hold beneath the skin
    The semblances of men,
    Blood runs in veins concealed.

Robins

Reminder of a world not of our making,
They have their own greeting,
Their own weeping,
Their privacy, custom and formality.

Winter compels their beggary at our doors,
But they as in court dress,
Stiff with apprehensive elegance,
Present to us their note for maintenance.

Snowdrops in March

Curious that these long-overdue February flowers
Should come almost unexpected to our
Remote world: and they suspensive in cold and light
Now remain even in their proper powers

Like a legend, dreamt of, not hoped on;
Nor for us, these, delicate, of perfect leaf
And petal, but secret hold
For other Springs their promissory note.

To a Child

An image on the sea's floor,
A plushy fungus, brine bubbled,
Will hold secure
(Breath and eyes untroubled),
From all uncertainties of choice
Every child that's suckled,
    And minister the fragrance
Of unstilled expectation
    And swim sweet surprise,
At every shimmer, to his eyes.

A Child Crying

The miserable moment
Breaks in your eyes
Breaks world, time, life in cries,
Spills all hope and pleasure upon the floor,
Tashes your body with the sore.

Fling a sunbeam in your eyes,
And frustrate every emblem of despair,
Cries to laughter, cries, cries, now laughter
Catch all morning air,
All sourness meadowfair.

A Young Girl

Bird eyes and voice ejaculate
Your comment
That flies uncaged
To us, stone-faced.

We watch your scattered notes
Ascend as rocket sparks
And fall like rain
On barren-ness.

Voyage We to Islands

Here is no continuing city
Voyage we then to islands in this
Flux of time and tide
And listen hoping for news beyond
Tide and time, and taste,
Anticipating the luscious long asked for
Fruit never withdrawn nor rotting.
A sun shines – but where?

From prints upon the brain,
Effluent into light, the tender past –
That seen by my childhood's eyes,
That which has long since withdrawn
On an ebb – flows now.
The rocking horse with glazed eye stares,
The cuckoo clock calls,
Its door shuts – these, part of a
Once for ever world, now once
Upon a time – gone with
The silver gong's stroke, fallen
From permanence.

Voyage we for islands securely pebbled,
Holding the boat's jar, time resistant,
With water diamonded under a white sun.
But where?

Homage to El Greco

The Agony in the Garden

Distant an unimportant soldiery,
(Those proscribed from bliss and agony
Living in worlds of space and time)
Sleepers, the garden of Gethsemane,
Depiction of His eyes and hands.

Look there in the garden
Where all shapes taken from
Hexagonal basalt to eruptive flame,
Prelude to the pattern
Of field and stream,
Retain, gather disruption,
Collect the flux of time and flame

To precipitate upon
The eyes that seek,
The hands that ask
The peace, the peace
Within the eyes that plead
The hands that speak,
The way, the life, the peace.

A Departure

The short man waves his hand,
Half turns, and then makes off.
He is going to the country
Taking the road with the field of clover
On one side, the beach on the other,
The beach jarred by white stones,
The clover globed waiting for soft winds.
At the top of the rise within earshot
Of both sea and birds for a moment
He stops. (Stop now for ever there
To witness sea sound, bird note,
Sea town's cries.) But he,
As if hurt and shamed,
Moves, head bent, clothes loose upon him.

We would offer blood, cash down,
For a last knowing gesture,
But the hill has him – or the sea.

Jute Spinner

What is it makes that shuttle fly?
Not ultimately the stroke of an uninformed engine,
Nor the subtle project of a capital enterprise.

What is it makes that shuttle fly?
Not a high voltage,
Nor current transmitted from a central store,
But every strand woven,
Every strand forced in
Warp and weft
Moves in its intricacy
From her nerves and bones and blood.

Epitaph for One Who Promised Well and Failed

'Perished on the first step of tomorrow.'
Who knows his own epitaph?
'His strength gathered between thumb and forefinger,
The pen prompt to the bidding of mind,
His nose snuffing the aesthetic possibilities of the violet,
Ears and eyes trained like old soldiers with a new recruit's spirit.'

Who knows his own epitaph?

The Sculptor

for T. S.Halliday

The man who handles
Bronze, clay, wood, stone,
Praises the durable,
Makes marble the moment.

Limbs, feature, muscle, palm,
The fine lines from the eye,
Supple back of animal,
(O make marble the moment!)

Bone, cheek, all tangible,
All touched by time,
Touched by the sculptor's art
Make marble the moment.

After Eden

My love, O, my love and I
Walked in a strange land.

Sun? – yes but blocked by the whitened mist,
Sea? – but known only by taste of salt,
Land? – the scent of clover told,
And sight gave, the field brightening beneath.

My love, O, my love and I
Walked in a strange land.

As robins do in a farm kitchen
Leaving momentarily prints on the stone flags,
Yet we different, our eyes turned within
To the fog that swirls at the eye sockets.

My love, O, my love and I
Walked in a strange land.

Hearing the sea swell that runs
Brain high and ebbs, leaving us a skull.
Our flowers sprout in our aches,
And shine from our dust.

My love, O, my love and I
Walked in a strange land.

Where, where is the homeland?
Which, which the blessed reality?
The foam crystalling on the bowsprit,
The image heaving on mortality?

Envoi

Go, drama of wind, water and stone,
Drama of men long under granite lid.
Go to those with abundant energy
Whose eyes lift to the hard North light.
Go to those shaken by the petulant sea.

A Man of Inconsequent Build and
Other Poems 1944–1964

A Man of Inconsequent Build[3]

In memoriam H.G.B. (1873–1941)

1.   For the few only, time has gifts,
   For most, ignoring her, crack.
   They cultivate a shell resistant
   To the taps, and willing deafness
   Hear no news of death or life
   Till at the brittle end.
   But for the choice few
   Participants, patient, unsheltered,
   And tender to the fine point;
   They have time's gifts.

2.   Almost bankrupted, business tied,
   The office held him to his chair,
   He sweated, hoped, lost heart,
   Yet through it noted his own suffering.
   And with this art the casual seas
   That made his trade, were legends.
   Babbled the jingling river stones,
   The flowers, that fringe the wave, stared out,
   Books with their different names
   And title deeds to recognition were grateful
   For his eye. His Odyssey the trains between
   Two ends of telephone; his giants competitors –
   But these became a man who limped,
   Or interesting because he'd news from other parts,
   Or held odd notions about signing cheques.

3.   The roads to the port struggle from their enclosures
   Down and flatten clear to the spatulate piers –
   Ten fingers of them seaward –
   And a long encircling wall to with-hold surge.
   To – fro in summer on a pier point coils
   Of horse-drawn lorries, klaxoned motor-power lorries
   Unwind in dust in a stretch up home
   To kipper sheds and yards, and down again.
   At the dead centre a man
   Manipulating the machinery of events
   Sucked so far within that shipmasts,
   The swinging arms, cursing ratchets,

The shafts of airward steam,
Shutter the sky: and within the small
office – business. A deal is struck
by phone with Mr Finklestein.
The market slips. None others knew
Bonded by words alone, it holds.

4.   High upon a three-legged stool the small man
With broad pale brow lined deep as if the pen
Held tight in hand had pressed its ink
In strokes. The office low-roofed, flaking plaster,
And he absorbed in computation stares on ink.
(Sleep, sleep the wound in the brain.)
A corrupting worm has fed upon the wood
Of stool and floor. He calculates. *(Sleep, sleep.)*
The low white light of morning breaks
With birds, and still his eyes reflect only
What the creatures of the day have seen,
The white, the red, the gray of dawn.
(Sleep, sleep the dust.)
Perilous, he pauses, ignorant of peril and,
With acetylene's force upon the steel, stares
On memory. *(Sleep the worm.)*
Eyes open on micaceous beach,
Islands assorted in their seas,
The air talk talks of gulls,
He stares without the pointed fear.
(Sleep, sleep the dust; the wound, the worm in the brain.)

5.   All held in a hand, all
Emanating from a head – God's Head,
Fish, antelope and star, held
And scattered each to his kind.
O to look equally on all, to stare
Even where His effulgence breaks in kind,
Bursts as a hurtling night
In a holocaust on a sail –
A boat broken on an ancient pier
With thrust of seeding water.
Did he learn to look
On jacket and sea-boot cast with plasm:
Watch in the beam of his intelligence
The worm in the chrysalis and the old

Woman on the stairs go from him,
And not regret their difference?

6. To see without fear, to be
A face in stillness. Latterly
Catarrhs, deafness, rheumatics occupied
His body; unconfined anxieties
Rummaged his tattered landscape.
Only his will remained in eyes
Time drawn. And then one day
The stuccoed ceiling gave, dissolved
To winter blue and in these airs
Becalmed perhaps he saw
The balance of his life – a gull
Remote and small, distinct and hovering,
Momentarily still with the apparent stillness
Of the distant waterfall; yet he at once
In the enjoyment of distance
And where his look fell,
Winged, equable, far seeing, benign, full,
As if had been projected from the body
The filled soul. He was there
Totally it and its difference.

Family Group

1. The wind blows
    I stare on memories
    As if each breath could resurrect
    The broken past.

    The wind blows
    Kindles the past –
    The town, street, room, bed.
    Head of my street –

    The spire in blue,
    And blown about the dusty street
    The crumpled dusty leaves
    The breath awakes from sleep.

2. Thus stood the father
    Hand on my shoulder,
    Thus the mother
    Arm wound about me.

    Did they ever move
    From the sepia
    Those in the staring days?
    Reined white horses

    Prance in the cold sun
    Father, mother, sister,
    Brother – sea-blown
    On the long prom.

3. Moved they ever!
    Ah pity, pity, pity,
    Cried I, at my entry
    Wept mother,
    My father in a far country.

Tom

1. TOM AND HIS TOYS

When I was small
I sat on the floor
For long, for long
And played with my golden ball.

The red engine and the black golliwog –
They sat and stared,
Stared at me till day
Dropped into the dark

That grew from the floor.
Then the tall mother moved
In the room with the great
Cupboard door. She said,

'Put them away –
The black golliwog, the red engine
And the golden ball –
Put them all away.'

She shut them in the cupboard
And never, never, never
Does the great door open,
Let them out, to stare so

As they did – this day, this night
For in the morning
I am a man.
The door does not open for the father.

2. TOM ON THE BEACH

With bent back, world's curve on it
I brood over my pretty pool
And hunt the pale, flat, sand-coloured
Fish, with cupped hands, in the cold.

Ah, but my warm heart, with hope
Wrapped in it in the bright afternoon
Feet glittering in the sand,
Eyes on my pale prey, was sure.

Suns have passed, suns have passed,
Skies purple above the thin sand.
With bent back brooding on the round
World, over my shoulder

I feel the touch of a future
In the cold. The little fish
Come not near me, cleaving
To their element and flattening on the sand.

How many years since with sure heart
And prophecy of success
Warmed in it
Did I look with delight on the little fish,

Start with happiness, the warm sun on me?
Now the waters spread horizonwards,
Great skies meet them,
I brood upon uncompleted tasks.

3. TOM IN BED

Tomorrow – in the steady afternoon
When the flat sand wrinkles miles
To the bleak monstered rocks
There I shall build my mountain

Of sand, and the red crab, the green crab,
The prickly spider crab will scramble over
And will awkwardly drop
Into the prepared pool on the other side.

That is what I will do with my spare time
And should have done so
Had not the suds of a thriving tide
  Pushed to my heels – and there

Behind me was the sea. And on it
The Ship – the Ship that for nights
Toppled about my bed
Carried its tarry business-like air,

Its barnacles and clammy sponges
To my nose and lips. My Ship!
My venture to be – but the invitation
Held hidden the knocking fist

If not carrion – and I would have plunged
Blanket wise but that the foam –
Brushed first life was there
Beneath in the child dark.

We hold out our hands to History
Then ask not to be taken.

4. Tom Discovers

On our cold summer afternoons the beaches were peopled.
Then when the mothers spread their rugs on the sand
To sit and knit the long day, when the kind sea
Washed to our waiting feet the tiny sea-creatures
Everything was simple and known – the pretty shells
In the green water were still, the painted pails contained
Enough water for the shallow pools. The sandwiches
And the tea-pots, the far-off gulls,
The houses and the churches and the factory chimney stood
In that air undisturbed, unmoving in the long afternoon.

But at night I would return to a different order
The sea withdrawn shrunken grey with a grey mud beneath
Lapping those rocks – not the blue rocks
The friends of the middle tides and every boy –
But those to be seen rarely – in moonlight I remember –
Loose and piled, scarred, splotched red and black
With green fingers of slithering weed.
Once I put my hand under the weed
Aged ten – a hand of ten years – to find
Time. And at night the mirror of the mind
Took up those towered and ancient rocks

With their unseen strength and depth
Of soft weed that swayed and turned
Persuaded by the mumbling tide!
O age, age, age and a world
Thundering to the insecure stars from a hand
But ten years gone from the womb.

Boys

1. IN A CROWD

Run –
In some corner boys, men will be
Picking up their heels; in almost any
Small town on the map of our island
On a bright cold summer Saturday,
In a sea-town going to the local football match
With a crowd of blue-trousered men, all
Stockily built and lean, some bearded,
Some blue chinned, going to the big game.
They walk on the crown of the tarred streets,
Hands dropping easily at sides, or in pockets
To clicking turnstiles, or in, if they're players,
At the big gate. And not a handsbreadth off
Sunday psalms; and always about their ears
Boats bobbing, cascades of herring.

2. SEEN DISTANT

The bird perches on the corroded machine,
The derelict machine in tall spindling grass
And the wind moves from the sand landward.
We were the shabby boys that edged the beach
Till night and watched the sea-light fail,
The sand blow draughty through our legs
And coil in puffs and leap and fall,
We blowing on our blue hands
And stamping on the shore.
The bird perches on the corroded machine
The derelict machine in tall spindling grass.

Fool and Cat

1. I drove in my engine
    Along the great street
    The crowds saw me coming
    And called it a feat

    The fool and the cat
    Come into their own.

    I counted the pennies
    I counted the gold
    I piled up the counter
    With bank notes untold

    The fool and the cat
    Come into their own.

    By code and by query
    I taught in a school
    I made them all judges
    By Zeus they could rule

    The fool and the cat
    Come into their own.

    I put out ten placards
    They came from afar
    They saw my gilt posters –
    My gold cinema

    The fool and the cat
    Come into their own.

    Then in came the couples
    And how they did stare
    My show was the best
    That ever was there

    The fool and the cat
    Come into their own.

They necked and they noodled
The manager smiled –
The banker, the judge, the teacher
Beguiled.

The fool and the cat
Come into their own.

O sweet are the lips
That grow on the screen
And pleasant the deaths
That are done in dream

The fool and the cat
Come into their own.

2.   My engine screams upon its side;
Who shouted in the darkening air?
A foul wind blows my notes about;
Who mocked at my despair?

The fool and the cat
Come into their own.

The Trinity

Time brought me a gold-eyed frog,
     A secretive snail, a squirrel,
A most delicate stepping high horse, and a hog,
     An ape and weasel.

Famine and drought and disbelief
     Now deny my sight
High horse and squirrel. A thief
     Took away my snail and frog.

Yet not the thickening at the eye
     Nor the thinning blood
Vanquish the trinity standing by,
     Ape, weasel and hog.

Proteus

When life breaks from the bone
Of the land, breaks in the dim
Morning, breaks in the hard known
Day, in the thin night wind,

Breaks as the heterogeneous,
Squalid, swarming plasm or
The single rock rose hid,
(Scenting a crannie's core,)

Breaks as the fact
Incredible – the babe –
Arriving in the sunless
Hut in the rubble.

Song for Elizabeth

Her young son singing
By her side,
Blackbird ringing
His sky-note high and wide –

Laughter over water
Where, where her heart lies
There singing sought her
Singing leaves and airs and tides.

Perfection

Upon the pausing air
The leaf dry and sere
In a momentary pause
Proclaims the good.

Cleave the wood
And the moment's halt
At the axe blade's fall
Proclaims the good.

Strike the stone
And the force that stood
A moment on the stone
Proclaims the good.

The moment of darkness
Falling on the air,
The moment of brightness
Rising on the air,

Halts to a poise
The beating blood,
The beating brain,
Proclaims the good.

66 South Street, St Andrews

An Elegy for Four Airmen

To this house, here
In this town
With the past
Like a blanket
Upon it, came

Four men, to be
Air-men, to do
What youth must.
(Has done these days
With wager, laugh
Or curse.)

This house –
Environed by study,
Immaculate study,
Slow-paced study –
Was *their* place.

One by one
The world-wide,
Hero-wanderers
Knew it
As home

As the moon grew,
First one;
As it waned
Another;
A third, in darkness;

A fourth – all
Into the unfair distances
Over the unkind islands
And waters, cloud storeyed
On windy ways,

To do what youth must
(These days)
Each to know
What age could not
Know.

Feather in the slip stream
Their bodies – this, only
This their discovery.
Vacancies between
The heart beats

Are greater, greater
Than the interstellar
Vacancies, greater
Than the

Outward eye conceives.
Heart convinced

Tomorrow was too far,
Each was hurried, rather
Slipped off his

Harness. Lord! what
Lonely days, months
Years in the moment
Beyond whose bound –

Now the deliberate four walls
Hold but memories. Four men
To be four air-men. All
Sweetness of life
In four known walls.

An Old and New Ruin

The towers by the years
Broken, are stained
By the sea's airs,
The airs that wind
About the arches,
The towers grown old
Fading upon the evening
With the sea-sound
About them; gently
The years winding
About them.

But the new
House was savaged,
A blemish; yet will it
So change, so alter
To be time-fit
No longer a halt,
The years closing upon it
Gifting the harmonies of ruin
The stillness of ruin.
Peace say the years
Peace in the stillness of the years.

A Gateway to the Sea (1)

At the East Port, St Andrews

Pause stranger at the porch: nothing beyond
This framing arch of stone, but scattered rocks
And sea and these on the low beach
Original to the cataclysm and the dark.

Once one man bent to the stone, another
Dropped the measuring line, a third and fourth
Together lifted and positioned the dressed stone
Making wall and arch; yet others
Settled the iron doors on squawking hinge
To shut without the querulous seas and men.
Order and virtue and love (they say)
Dwelt in the town – but that was long ago.
Then the stranger at the gate, the merchants,
Missioners, the blind beggar with the dog,
The miscellaneous vendors (duly inspected)
Were welcome within the wall that held from sight
The water's brawl. All that was long ago.
Now the iron doors are down to dust,
But the stumps of hinge remain. The arch
Opens to the element – the stones dented
And stained to green and purple and rust.

Pigeons settle on the top. Stranger,
On this winter afternoon pause at the porch,
For the dark land beyond stretches
To the unapproachable element; bright
As night falls and with the allurement of peace,
Concealing under the bland feature, possession.
Not all the agitations of the world
Articulate the ultimate question as do those waters
Confining the memorable and the forgotten;
Relics, records, furtive occasions – Caesar's politics
And he who was drunk last night:
Rings, diamants, snuff boxes, warships,
Also the less worthy garments of worthy men.

Prefer then this handled stone, now ruined
While the sea mists wind about the arch.

The afternoon dwindles, night concludes,
The stone is damp unyielding to the touch,
But crumbling in the strain and stress
Of the years: the years winding about the arch,
Settling in the holes and crevices, moulding.
The dressed stone. Once one man bent to it,
Another dropped the measuring line, a third
And fourth positioned to make wall and arch
Theirs. Pause stranger at this small town's edge –
The European sun knew those streets
O Jesu parvule; Christus Victus, Christus Victor,
The bells singing from their towers, the waters
Whispering to the waters, the air tolling
To the air – the faith, the faith, the faith.

All this was long ago. The lights
Are out, the town is sunk in sleep.
The boats are rocking at the pier,
The vague winds beat about the streets –
Choir and altar and chancel are gone.
Under the touch the guardian stone remains
Holding memory, reproving desire, securing hope
In the stop of water, in the lull of night
Before dawn kindles a new day.

St Andrews, June 1946

Old tales, old customs and old men's dreams
Obscure this town. Memories abound.
In the mild misted air, and in the sharp air
Toga and gown walk the pier.
The past sleeps in the stones.

Knox in his tower, bishop and priest
In the great cathedral, a queen's visit –
All traditional currency. Once there was
Meaning in the formula, gesture implied
Act. Now where's the life of the town?

Concurrence of event and sentiment
Confound perception! But look!
A small boat brings its morning catch,

Haddock and cod, plaice and mackerel.
Good sales! Landladies, hotels, hostelries,

Housefull! And America walks the street.
Today the train's spilling its complement
Down windy lanes to restaurants,
And afternoon — the beach, queues for
Cinema – or golf all day. Night –

History shrieks from the stones,
Knox, Douglas and Wishart,
Prison and torment.
Blind the eyes, broken the heart
Knox, Douglas and Wishart.

Good Wishes for a Departure

To Jean, my sister

Town now step into your heart –
From the fine white rabbit's skull
At the sea's edge, sea-beaten and wind searched
To the faces of men set by storm
And the hope of a haven hereafter.

Now let the misted harbour with distanced sounds,
The intermittent hooves and wheels,
The sudden vibration of the night fog-horn,
The lighthouse beam stalking about your room,
The night winds at the granite corners,

Let them all now enter subtly
And settle lightly (for these were home)
And be an air within your mind.
Once you were the girl waving goodbye
To us the way-going brothers.

Now your journeys. May all the echoes
That collect in shells, and all the ancient
Sea-sounds of the town – adding your personal care,
The moment of the puppy's bliss bearing your shoe –
Be yours unfading and without tears.

In Praise of Henry Moore's 'Pink and Green Sleepers'

To penetrate the fuss, the shelter stir and threat,
The steamy cocoa, electric words and flickering thought
Of those who moved, raised protecting arms, or slept
And to arrive, behind the eyes, at what
Had but been guessed, was his historic bent.
He looked and noted, bringing home
The calm of rock. Was this his end –
Encrusting like the frost at the pace
Of aeons, or was the human rest
Deeper, quieter than created stone?
He looked and noted, leaving us sleepers larger
Than our aches, more lasting than our dreams.

An Island and Seals

Old grey heads, curious and stupid like the old
They came about our anchored boat
Wondering at us visitors to their ancient world
Of tides and beaches peopled with fish and birds.
On the white sands the spindly oyster catchers,
In the shallows the frantic terns,
Above the mast the heavy black-backed gulls –
All considered us, took our measure.

Every would-be traveller – and who is not?
Must at the first dawn-streaked sky
Step with hope – or heartless – East, West, South or North.
Seas are between, land or doubtful sky
And painful traverse sets in motion
Heart beats to an ancient tune. Time
For a departure. O Time! One it is alleged
Once sought successfully but with too much pain.

There was a pause, a cessation of motion,
A pause in the bobbing grey heads, a pause
In the motion of water. Light fixed
The red-legged oyster catchers, caught

Black-capped tern and lumbering gull
In an equipoise. We looked beyond
To island upon island linked in the long
Glittering of waters – wondering where?

Now in the years between I doubt
If all was well on that bright day.
Had we but kept the bounded measure,
Ceased from willing, observation, conversation
With the self and with another,
Had we but simply been at leisure
In that suspense of fish and bird and sea
And with the old grey-headed seals – what then?

The Rowan Tree

Where drops the pebble silent to the sea
Where red moor tufts cliff edge
Under remorseless heaven in a chill
There spreads my silent love – O rowan tree.

At this cliff edge on the flat stone
With a little soil, open to the chafing gale
Hurt by the cruel and biting salt
There spreads my silent love – O rowan tree.

Summer ends its straining light
Blood drops pendant in the yellowing sun
Harsh leaves hanging to the chilling moon
There spreads my silent love – O rowan tree.

Touched by the calculating winter mists
Cursed by obscure and beaten seas
A derelict struck by fierce frosts
There spreads my silent love – O rowan tree.

As waters halt at this cliff base
Welter and shock inviolable stone
So you – as grasp your tough roots rock –
Halt here the heart – O rowan tree!

Sumburgh Heid[4]

Rummle an' dunt o' watter,
Blatter, jinkin, turn an' rin –
A' there – burst an' yatter
Sea soun an muckle an' sma win
Heich in a lift clood yokit.
Heich abune purpie sea, abune reid
Rocks – skraichs. That an' mair's i' the dirdit
Word — Sumburgh, Sumburgh Heid.

The Old Fisherman

Girn and clash ye gangrel seas
An sough ye wun
We wha fran yer mell tak ease
Loup good herrin, loup good codlin
Noo hae done.

Skirl and yammer ower the steens
An skraich ye wun
The boatie's tae the pier heid teen
Loup good herrin, loup good codlin
We hae done.

Rax, carfuffle, shift an sweir
An brak ye lift
I wha vrocht sair i the steer
Loup good herrin, loup good codlin
Noo hae done.

But oh! – the raucle ocean's sweet
An sweet the wun
To his wha frae their ploy took meat
Loup good herrin, loup good codlin
I hae done.

Late Springs this North

Late springs this North and Spring
Is cold with sea-borne air.
Wind bursts in the wide country.
By dyke and ditch the whins flare
Hares leap in the new ploughed furrs
Folk gang at the business that's theirs.

> *Andra and Jockie*
> *Scutter wi the tractor*
> *Jean's i the kitchie*
> *Dod's i the byre*
> *Fred the orra loon*
> *Chops kindlin for the fire.*

Late springs this North, hard the sun,
Caller the wind that blows to the bone.

Fingal's Cave

Eye does not penetrate but ear records
From the inner wall even the susurrus of motion,
And subtle sounds elaborated by smoothed pillars
Are orchestra with wind fall and rise,
Interlaced with murmur, knock, drive,
Shock, upon stone, and all echo, echo, echo in a vault.

Thump, your boat will end herself here
As well as on a wide sea.
Cry your heart will hear its own
Cry here as well as on a mourning day.
Call – call of bone, bird, earth, water, air
And stone in a pillared west coast cavern here.

Valediction for Henry Moore 1944

1.   In stone and in the subtle pencil line
      The Word was yours – this moment
      Was yours, making of the shapes of war
      That tumble up the telescope end
      With limbs, hair, staring eyes – one thing
      To contemplate, to be borne.[5]
      The word was yours to look upon
      The long shelter perspective to know
      This is what I or Europe am become
      And no truce will dissuade the dark.
      Some in the corridor will move, some sleep,
      Some raise protecting arms to waive
      What is already there within. The pain
      Is that on all – he who by main force
      Lifted the rigid back and leaned upon the hand,
      And she who slept, and he who
      Too far within the tube to be seen
      Distinctly, whether lying prone, supine
      Or propped within the concave wall,
      On all the cold insists.

      O Sun (Son of God) what word to restore
      From anonymity restore to diversity.
      What pain to awake the numbed and hooded.
      As the blood flows to the frosted limb
      Will the sun now touch those,
      The vindictive, the denatured, the desperate,

2.   The eyeless, the indifferent, all who
      So long ago were bereft of the garden?
      Beneath the ruined moon the stone sleepers
      In their countries misted with the delicate yellow dust
      That sifts under the nails and lies at the nostrils.
      Once the vague wind broke upon their moving thighs.

      The present is never wholly evil
      The past is never wholly good
      And at this moment in the dissipation,
      In the movement towards no place,
      Towards no end, with no time in mind,
      There is the image.

3.   Summon to the mind the living image.
The running figure on the fine day,
The boy amongst boys on the broad beach
The hands at the herring shaken to the hold.

And each states I am the past
As the receding daylight arc of the tunnel
These are complete and apart:
And each states I am the past.

And the command is – define, encompass
This not that, now not then, the eccentric,
The dubious, the moving, lips shaping,
Seek the images that waylay the years.

The tree in the garden, the figure
Transfixed in Time, the babe,
The parting of raiment:
Christus Victor in the garden –
The images that waylay the years:
And trust that they will set down
Time and place, this day and this place.

4.   This day and this place,
And unto Adam he said
Cursed is the ground for thy sake
In sorrow shalt thou eat of it
All the days of thy life.
Thorns also and thistles
Shall it bring forth to thee
And thou shalt eat the herb of the field
In the sweat of thy face shalt thou eat bread
Till thou return unto the ground
For out of it wast thou taken
For dust thou art
And unto dust shall thou return.

The stones were lifted from the fields
The animals driven to their holes, the land
Drained, dug, planted, the ground pieced out.
The heather was beat: the crop grew
On the hill. The paths were trod,
The people were upon the land.

> *My love, O my love and I*
> *Walked in a strange land.*

Sun! but blocked by the whitened mist
Sea? but known only by the taste of salt
Land? the scent of clover told
And sight gave the field brightening beneath.

> *My love, O my love and I*
> *Walked in a strange land.*

Hearing the swell that runs
Brain high and ebbs.
Where, where is the homeland?
Which, which the blessed reality?

> *My love, O my love and I*
> *Walked in a strange land.*

To go down the years thus,
To dwindle in the narrowing perspective!
I saw two and about them
The rocks stood from the ground.
A bird flew up.
In the passage the coulter was in the soil
There were two
And one with a backward look.

> *My love, O my love and I*
> *Walked in a strange land.*

5. Homage to him who reports the kingdoms of the dead,
    The place of the desert and the fire and the convulsion.
    Homage to him who sets down the moment of tears,
    Who carefully notes those bowed, those broken
    Those estranged, those contorted by violence, those waiting,
    For a new day. We are a homely people
    Who fear the night, remembering only
    The day when the rose bloomed in the silent sun
    Or the moonlit evening on the beach with the sea
    Lifting its fringes flowerlike, falling and lifting,
    Or the visit of friends to tea to talk of friends.

    > *My love, O my love and I*
    > *Walked in a strange land.*

    We desire no more than that each thing
    Be as it appeared to be those years before.
    Your too accurate eye makes all legend.
    The bear grunts in his mountain. The ice moves.
    Slowly the sap gathers to the vegetation.

O do not wake us from our sleep
With new dreams in the drumming sky.
Let the old year go in our sleep.
Valediction for an old bad year.

The Seaman, an Epilogue

For Andrew Stewart

What vision his. Northward he stares
On polar suns that burst and flood
On black and blood-red water
Whose movement breaking the white light
Prismatically, spreads North and North
Salt gold and green to the cold berg's foot.

What vision his when South he looks
From sea to land, across those waterways –
Home, seen now in the perspective of space,
Men minute and shadow-like, active at their doors,
Pulling their doll-like crafts ashore.
He sees their purposes, yet hears nothing,
No pebbles' jar, no thump of boat, no shout
As rapid waters easily o'erwhelm
And run about the low decks and thrust
Aside the boats, returning them to the original sea.

Yet *he* trusting these shadows,
More real than rock, hearts perdurable
Without doubt or fear – homeward steers.

The Helmsman

Write out the wind of his hometown
And reckon its dance, not as the impact
On a wall, but on his history.

> *This wind that killed in the desert*
> *That slit the ice-cap,*
> *That blasted first life from soil,*
> *That chanted about the Inn at night,*
> *Blew winter at the Babe;*

Blows to a flare the light in any
Hero helmsman's brain till his head
Above its circles – hands on wheel –
Is circled by a cloudless constellation.
His eyes are stars, his arms embrace
An unhinged world. Astride the swelling wind
In the empty dawn, in the horizon light
He becomes stature.

The Singers

O Thalassa! Thalassa! Where, where
Are the winged instruments of celebration!
Where are the singers of today?
We did not know that our sea, debauched
By old men's pilferings, sullied by paddling boys,
Was not unsimilar to Homer's ocean,
Our bitter, treacherous coast reminiscent.
We did not know the music of the Ancient World
Whispered with the spindrift at our back door,
Offered its strange acclamation with wintry thunderings
For all who would hear. But we
Would not, could not, had no eyes for the dawn,
No ears for the wavering music of the wind.

> *The porridge pot is on the fire,*
> *The spelding's frae the rack,*
> *Or we can catch the tide at five*[6]
> *Ower meat we maun be swack.*

> *Charlie's at the pier lang syne*
> *Tae fuel engine an test her.*
> *Hist ye. Meg, the baited lines*
> *And hist ye, lass, ma s'wester.*

'The rosy-fingered dawn' – we had no eyes for the dawn –
And the music was there waiting.
Years back – when the sun only was light
And the dark lit only by the night fires
The music waiting the singers of love and violence
Of our country, with the coasts
Fringed with the lifting and falling of waters
With the wide unmarked straths and narrow glens,
The country of the ancient inviolable rock
The music waiting for the singer
To tell the tale at the roaring night fire
To send it forward into the unborn future.

> *Drap the anchor, Charlie! Dod,*
> *We're tee the gruns noo*
> *If but the weather'll only haud*
> *We'll full the boxes foo.*

> *But gin she blaw anither bittock*
> *Or shift a pint to North*
> *Nae one whiting, cod or haddock,*
> *Nae a maik we're worth.*

Here the rock-strewn shore and the swift tide
Breaking the timbers of the laden boat:
Here a land of rock and little soil
But held from the invader.
What is won with difficulty is twice ours
And twice over again worthy of song,
And the songs are with the black-capped tern
On the wide waters and with the swinging gull
In the rebuffed wind. Songs
In a land of the strange and the common –
The irregular crags in the green winter light,
The frozen fall in the secret corrie,
The caves with the sounding waters,
The caves of the dying birds,
The hollow hills and the deadly currents

And the slow sun rising on the ordinary landscape.
The country of low stone dykes and tractable fields,
The man at his labour in the field,
The obedient dog, the sheep on the low hill.
The woman at the baking board,
The children with blue butterflies in the hard sun
On the road to the shore.
A boy with a can of milk walks to the shore,
Returns with shining herring to the dark land.

> *Throttle her doon, Dod*
> *At thon black rock*
> *Tide's runnin' strang, Dod*
> *We'll coup gin she knock.*

> *A sait tyave it wis, boy*
> *In yon black swell,*
> *But we're hame wi' a shot, boy*
> *Will dee us well.*

In the cold of morning – as day
Stretches on the hills – the beginning,
The resumption of the tasks of the day –
The woman moving about the house,
The child crying, the cattle heaving
In their stalls. The boat goes from the pier,
The wind creeps to the wide waterways,
The ploughman drives the long furrow.
And in the prime of day – activity.
By the road to the shore in the sun
The sheep's backs are dappled with sweetness
Happiness spreads like summer.
At night the world is in the mouths of men –
Till the flames are down and the embers ash.

> *Lat go that rope, loon,*
> *Watch, she'll brak,*
> *Smert's the word, loon,*
> *Or she snap.*

> *Alec John's deid.*
> *Ae weet nicht*
> *Slipped, cracked his heid,*
> *Pitten oot in sma' licht.*

Our coasts have no laurels – only the white dawn.
Yesterday the seas cavorted, brought
With the thin spume, Alec John's blue mitt.
Yesterday a fankled line took Sandy,
A pot in the wrinkled sand foundered Jock Bayne.

To salvage *The Water Lily* was a fikey business –
The crew were all young men.
We did not know as the tides came upon us
And our rivers ran in spate to the sea
Our waters were touched by the Athenian sun.
Where, where are the singers,
Where the winged instruments of celebration?

Gateway to the Sea (2)

Corraith, built 1871. Innellan

This was his dream. To anchor in Time
Where the fierce salt was softened by the rose.
Spindly wrought-iron gates would welcome the wide sea,
Peace would sail into his Victorian calm,
Befriend his pale city children.
All was as he imagined.
The waters brimmed beyond the gates,
A mild surf beckoned the lilies,
The croquet lawn whispered its conversation
To the waters. The yucca prospered
In the Scottish air. This sleight of hand
That conjured four white horses,
Landau, paddle boat and the band,
Waltz and polka and the parasols
On the lawn, could it sustain
The tea-rose and the hushed waters,
Convert the embattled submariners,
Cuttlefish and crab and the sub-lit world?

Evening chimed from the mantleshelf,
The whorled shells gathered the echoes,
Roses spread upon the water,
Serenely gazed from the waters,
The faces of children looked at themselves
Sails reached up from sails.

Church and house, pier and paddle steamer
Lay tenderly there. Would this pass
With the proper way of taking tea,
With the knowledge of the right answers,
With the words not to be spoken,
And History prevail,
The jungle ocean ravage garden
And house, clad hill
And the parasols, the stock-brokers
And the tea-merchants – to leave
But a stone, a stone to say
Yes to Time?

In our day
We visited the place. It stood
With the slight green gates
At the end-of-the-world moment,
And not a parasol, not a polka.
And the whorled shells gathered
The evening light and the sea sound
To themselves in air like silk.
Was this moment another dream?

Through the glass's healing eye
Each and every to his kind,
The mauve-grey turtle heaving by
Each and every as his mind.
The star-fish to his rock,
Common crab with his rock face,
Staring cod and Peter's haddock,
Each to his appointed place
Classical leviathan here contained;
All signatories to the pact –
Content to be sustained
By a single mental act.

Fishermen's Cliff Houses[7]

Blind backs to the blind sea;
Something was being said by them
In their silence, while the wind blurted about
Their stone corners that stood on stone,
And the muffled talk of waters
Fell from those shut windows.
Nothing given away about the life
That must have been, must be there
Still in the dark that moved
Inside the place awaiting return.

The rock-rose opens on the rock,
Shooting light to light.

Seaman, fisherman, who do not return
To the waiting dark, you wait now
The light of the Galilean sea to break
Like a flower on your brain again.

Cheery Sam

Gull, negligent swinging, weighting wings
On an air current over black water
In slow swell, unbroken, empty. Buffet
Hurls upwards, pressures move aside
Low in a slip-stream of air.
In that gold-orbed questionless eye
That feeds promiscuously on light,
Clean, clear or dwindling ambiguous,
The spectrum ranges from black purpling
To green water where protrudes
Skeletal remains, ship-ribs; a strake
Rakes skywards with one broad traverse
Hammered with rusty bolts – The RUBY –
Gone in the dark. Of her crew, Sam only
Was drowned and he, deep in drink,
Had glowed in many sunsets in the bar;
His jewelled accordion shone with stars.
His music mixed with the racketing winch.

'Hup!' he bawled from the slithering hold,
His thigh boots deep in squeaking herring.
Basketed he swung them skywards. 'Hup!'
And 'Never fecht your meat, man.'
These were his words. Sam had no quarrel
With words or man or self
But with the port bow. Clumsy he slipped
Cracked his bald cranium; clean out,
But rose again – will do so no more.
Cheery Sam played the bloody squeeze box
To the moon. Now silent, salted,
He stares from all that drink.
Gull ignorant as nature, surveys,
Perches on the garboard strake.

Landscapes and Figures[8]

1.   Whinbush, wind-beaten, flares summer.
      One statement of colour only against
      Rain-leaden sky, in lea of a low dyke
      In rock land and salt pasture
      To the round of sea. Nothing more.
      No grace here, nor riches, but authority.
      Here the single lark sings in the brain
      (Curtailment of life by the astringent salt),
      The weasel in the wall gestures at the raging
      Hare making fast for, its only month, March.
      Frozen in Time they utter a way
      No less than Van Gogh's chair,
      Shabby with pipe and ash upon it,
      And no more.
            Here is authority.

2.   Present now an island with multitude,
      A hundred songs at once bursting the air
      With larks, tumbling pee-wits till moonrise
      Where orchis lights pink, blood-red and purple
      The black moors, rimmed by the imponderable sea.
      In this theatre the ruined arch, the stone
      Steps worn by the pious and the impious

To the altar and the kitchen. Oysters
And golden amontillado for the abbot,
Brown beer for the other orders.
Between the rose-garden and the rhubarb patch
The runnel grosses the kitchen fats
And through the slits in the containing wall
Out of the castle on the hill, the bulk
Of life, the visiting soldiery come
(From time to time engendering the village)
To accept the benedictions of the cross.
Proliferation, cruelty, processionals,
Motley and some grace.

3.　　All gone to rack-ruin: what with
　　　Invasion, reformation, deformation,
　　　Mildew, neglect, mould, persistence
　　　Of air, water, heat, cold, damp,
　　　Mere absence of persons until
　　　The Ministry of Works clocked in
　　　(St Aidan, St Cuthbert looked from
　　　The priory to the herring sea).
　　　'Two bob a time,' said the guide,
　　　'Climb the wall, that's what the bastards
　　　Do. Set foot on hallowed ground –
　　　That's their carry on, 'less I nip round.'
　　　Two crows sit on the arch that branched
　　　And broke the thin blue sky.
　　　'Two crows! That's 'em back
　　　That stole St Cuthbert's new straw thatch,'
　　　The guard from the castle bawls;
　　　'Not Sundays, Thursday's opening day,
　　　Pubs open Sunday – all day, all day.'
　　　Shuttered from the sun the soldiers
　　　Push their dominoes on marble tops.
　　　The coaches roar upon the beach.
　　　The girls go gay in dolly hats, ribald
　　　The toy trumpets shriek, a feast
　　　For Bob, Tom, John. Lit up
　　　They swelter in the westering sun.
　　　Tonight the red-gold horses call
　　　With klaxon music from the stalls.
　　　A few spill over on the abbey grass,

Tom Jenkins having one too many.
Early this mild September dark
Sets in. Soundless the sea encroaches,
Salt encrusts the lovers and the rose.
Forgotten on the sand two children play,
They build an abbey with a future
That crumbles at the touch of tide.

The Island

The water was glass and the little fish
Sported above the clear sand.
The sunflashed ripples shot a hundred
Blisses and the boat barely nodded
Yes to plenty. This was their land.

Yesterday we visited the island
Returned to tern, gull, rabbit and plover
After the occupation by another kind,
Righteous, bearded and blue-chinned men,
Curers and fishers and women to work at the herring.

Piers grew. Hammers split the screaming
Of terns. Barrels roistered down the braes –
Empties to be stuffed with herring
By Lil, Nell, Bell, Teenie and Jeannie.
Jew and Gentile were welcome to this island.

Fifty years ago old George Bruce[9]
(Top hat packed, in case, just in case)
Shovel beard but gentle, a short man,
Pale eyed, considering mind,
Active on his pins, stumped this island.

And it was good – all was good.
(Kirks were in his waistcoat pocket
Ready for planting, pandrops
White as sea-washed pebbles ready,
But not – not to be 'sooked' at sermon.)

Britannia on her brown penny
Ruling the waves and justice
Walking on the beaches in a
Black frock-tailed coat;
Law, order and some good humour

And a minimum o' sweirin
Mainly frae Chairlie wha played
A squeeze box, wheezy – a wee thing –
Wi saut watter in't, played it
For the lassies to gie them speirit.

And all was work! All a-slithering
Red-eyed, salt-scaled glut of herring
Basketed, swung by ratchet, hand winched
From hold to hands bobbing at barrels
Lil, Bell, Jean, Teenie – ho! Nellie.

Oily oilskins, a-speckle with, shot with
Blood bright scales; brine fed herring
Neat, exact packed. And elbow deep
In herring, head, arms, back in a barrel
Jeannie, Teenie, Bell, Nellie.

Bottoms up. 'God', says Chairlie
'Yon quines!' – but old George Bruce –
And all was work. Barrels dunt and deave
Till peace laps the strakes of the fat steamer
Leaving the late evening air of the island

And the girls and the gulls and the wooden
Pier. 'Wood', said George Bruce, 'is not enough'
And built stone. The occupation
Was zenith. The milkwort skies
Took the thundering hammers to themselves.

The roister of barrels in the heavens,
The language of Chairlie in the heavens,
Wisps of tow in the heavens,
The faint twist of smoke –
All gathered to the heavens.

(As he left his fortifications
A little wind blew about his beard,
A white handkerchief from the stern,
Frock-coated he waved farewell.)
'Maister's for hame,' said Chairlie.

I found no trace of him, nor others.
The cold sun treated with the present
Occupiers, fish and birds. Terns
Inhabited the stone pier, a vantage
For sallies to the transparent water

Through which we sailed gently
Yet with more disturbance than proper
Dispersing that other order that contained
Thump and scream, roar and the faint
Birth cries of what was to become.

Advance party we were of the new
Sought for stability, had come to treat
With the politic world, the darkened
World. The cathode tube, our friend,
Was tunnelled in the concreted rock.

Antennae we were to the welded
State, invested with authority to
Dispose in chemistry, defecate to
Transparency sand, rock, bowels
Of earth such as improperly impeded

Arrangement. Guaranteed by equation,
By knowledge of the violent heart of
The matter, we sat encased in
Our transparent silence. Nothing
Could stir but was seen, heard,

Known as the movement of the hand
Is known. Distance was nothing,
Desire ordered by necessity. The rare
Jewel of single, systematised thought
Empired in the nodalled brain.

Use, the beauty of it, frictionless
And therefore never spent, a new
Kind of immortality in a muscled
Relation of instrument to instrument,
Electron to electron, thought to –

Thought of the incredible chance of
ORDER. Now grandfather praised
God for a solid demonstration
Of his order and we, can we
Praise among the irregular stars,

Praise the solitary mind that moved
From the blessed time when
The blackbird disputed the hawthorn
To tomorrow slit by knowledge,
Damned by the colding dark?

Doubt tunnels rock like wood-worm,
Makes short work of the long argument of love.
(From the springy bough of the lime tree
Her song falls to the breeding soil,
O my love dwelt in a far country!)

Doubting on a northern island
I, the antennae of the race,
Cigarette glowing beneath the lid
Of night seek a lost word
Can the lips shape 'Bless, O blessed'.

Aberdeen, the Granite City

The brown land behind, south and north
Dee and Don and east the doubtful sea,
The town secured by folk that warsled
With water, earth and stone; quarrying,
Shaping, smoothing their unforgiving stone,
Engineering to make this sufficient city
That takes the salt air for its own.
The pale blue winter sky, the spring green trees,
The castigating thunder rain, the wind
Beating about the midnight streets,
The hard morning sun make their change
By the white unaltered granite –
Streets of it, broad roadways, granite pavemented
To the tall tenements, rectangular wide-walled stores,
To the kirks and pillared Assembly Rooms;[10]
Streets with drinking troughs for the animals,
And at the port quays crowded,
Overfed with horses, lorries, men and boys,
And always and at every point
Clatter on the causies.
Business is good, will be good here
At the dead end of time. Record then
This people who purposive and with strategy
Established a northern city, a coast town
That stands and stares by the waters,
Dee and Don and the sea.

Praising Aberdeenshire Farmers

Thin ice glazing summer grass;
Here the red rowan is filched from the bough
By the cracking wind.
Sap freezes in the cold sun.

This is the East coast with winter
Written into its constitution
And so is very productive of men
Who do not wait for good
In case there is none.

They know their shortening day
Drops quick into night.
Their confidence is in knowledge
Got under duress, so
They have developed that
Deliberating and acquiring mind
That comprehends facts, and acts.

Let us praise them.
They have made the land good.

Their fat lambs dance on green pastures
That run to rock ridges,
Milch cows graze on rock top,
Sap where was perished grass
They have made the land good.
Life where was none. Praise them.

Houses and Other Poems

1964–1970

Visitations from a War-time Childhood

1.   Of the five waiters, white, stiff-shirt fronted
With silver trays on the tips of fingers,
At the ready with napkins as white
As their paper faces,
Four were perfect.

     The fifth had a shoe-lace untied.

     His waxwork tear at his eye
Registered discomfiture,
Conveyed his regret to the single customer
In the corner.

     The naphthalene lighting placed the scene;
Edwardian. One
Should not shop at this restaurant
Longer than need be
But pass on to carnage.

2.   1914.
He returned in 1917,
His legs bandaged in khaki,
His boots shining new polished.
Marvellous how he had got rid of the trenches.

     The only reminder
Was the thin red line at his throat.

3.   Now when big-brother Arthur
Stepped
Over our granite doorstep
With his soldier's Balmoral
In his hand

     And we had shut the door
On the bright sea
That customarily roared
Outside
And he stood there waiting

For the mother to say
'You're home and no different'.
And the jolly father
To say
'How many Boche this time?'

I put up my finger
To touch the warm flesh
Of the hero who had
Actually killed
A man

And in a good cause.

But there was no difference
In that hand.

That August the beaches with their waves
Sang their habitual songs.

4.   O tide of no particular moment,
     Mumbling inconsequences to the pink feet of little girls,
     With the hot sun on the newspapers
     Beneath which soft snoring fathers puff,
     And the mothers knitting for dear life –
     Life not yet entered on the scene
     Or about to leave; content
     Spilling with the sand pies on the beach,
     Sporting with the swimmers in the ocean,
     In the afternoon cups of tea gossiping
     To the dull air; in this fixed
     Security without height or depth or thought
     Let the grandmothers, mothers, fathers and little children
     Be no more than themselves – sufficient,
     (Sufficient unto the day is the evil thereof.)
     As the beach rescue throws out his chest,
     As the diver cleaves the confident air,
     As the billows of great Aunt Isa
     Flow into and over the deck chair –
     On this simple day – Hallelujah!

5.   In those days
    War used to be kept
    Decently, as Aunt Isa said
    (Like the servants)
    In its place

    Out there . . . out there.

6.   'Oot there, oot there.'
    Joe said,
    'A whale's blawn; herrin's
    There. Helm's doun.' Joe said.

    'Haud on,' Jock said,
    'Ye've cloured ma heid
    On thon damned winch;
    Watter ships at speed.'

    'Niver fecht y'r meat, lad,
    There's aye them that's waur.
    Alec got his leg aff
    Tween a gunwale an a wa.

    There's herrin oot there, lad,
    Siller for the takin:
    Whaur's the spunk in ye, lad?
    Ye hinna y'r father's makin.'

    'Muckle gweed it did ma Da,
    An him V.C. an a'.
    He mine sweeped the channel,
    But they couldna sweep his banes awa.'

7.   Fortunately they recovered
    The body of the commander.
    The Union Jack fluttered a little
    As the waters enclosed the coffin.

8.   Jockie said tae Jeannie,
    'In ma wee box, in ma wee box,
    D'ye want tae see
    Fit's in ma wee box?'

'Siller preens for lassies
An a gowd locket for me,
That's fit ye've got
In your wee box.'

'In ma wee box, in ma wee box
's a German sailor's finger a' worn awa
Chawed by the sharks
Till it's nae there ava.'

Dunt gaed the gun
At eleeven o' the clock,
Up gaed the rocket
An the war's a' done.

9.   And the Lord God said,
Can these bones live?
For the land is full of bloody crimes,
The city full of violence.

The Red Sky

Till that moment the church spire
At the top of our street was encased
In that blue sky. Occasionally white
Puffclouds drove straight to heaven.
At the foot of our street
The Central Public School, granite,
Also encased in blue.
We lived in between with the
Worms, forkies, shell-fish, crabs –
All things that crept from stones,
And with the daisies for company.
Each was alive and very worthy,
Just right, till I met
The curly boy with the square shoulders
Who knocked me down
Pushing his fist into my teeth.
Then a crack ran though the red sky.
From then on it was never the same.

Child on the Beach

On the shore a child picked up
The bleached skull of a rabbit,
Noted the empty eye socket,
Then ran with his joy
Till this dead shell halted
His step to hear at his ear
Miracles shout from cavities
That contained seas at work.

But age picked on me that day.
The ear was blank at that hole.
The dance of all the fishes stopped,
The tern dived oh not for fun,
The sea shrunk grey and unimportant.
Listen, be attentive to the years.
Note the thin bone structure,
Salt entered the eyeholes
To make this new thing.

The Child and the Sea

1. THE BETRAYAL

But the firm sand betrayed her
And the ball spinning was caught
By the shivering sea.
Treacherous it danced her heart
Took it to its perplexity in an endless
Time streaming horizonwards.

Nor would again the flaunting sun
Tell truths of happiness to be,
Nor would those disturbed waters
Entrusted with a hundred confidences
Receive her benediction; kindnesses
Would not grow from her lips again.

The dream was taken from her.
She was no more herself. Once
The blue pebbles at the edge
Of the lemonade sea were sweets.
How many years had it held
In hiding this unsupportable moment.

2. SHE REBUKES THE SEA

O my love, once you were tremendous
With a billion wonders to tell,
Tell me of tales of thin finned
Angels that went about my
Pearly feet in the sand
That snuggled the brazen
Faced crabs with pop-eyes.
Once, my love, you sent
The bubbles gold-eyed to the top.
Salt you were, you, more blissful
Than candies with your sharp
Tongue. But you
Were with the unkind Time
That took the world
To the grudging night.

Blind Old Man

In the cold spring sun
the old man sits at the door
waiting for renewal as sturdy
crocuses make way for other tubers –
narcissi. A girl lightfoot
passes him without a sign,
wordless, hurrying to byre.
The cows are waiting warm
for her pail. Outside a small boy
pokes in the ditch for spawn.
The brilliant sky shafts
the crackling branches. Dust
curls upwards to chestnut buds.

A lark wastes song in the sky.
Day diminishes. Under
the palm of the old man
words run to his fingers,
live in his blood
warmer than summer.

Butterfly

at Rubislaw Quarry

That blue day, when the white dust paused
in the air as the chisel fissured
granite block – quarried to outlast decay,
I remember a blue butterfly
that rose from dry grasses,
lifted airy over granite edge,
over corroded machine, over chasm,
in the beam of the sun – gone.

Every moment is goodbye to every moment
but the beam of the mind holds butterfly.

Explorers

1.   He rode tall into the hot sun
      over the raw-grained sand
      amongst the shattered rocks
      that at first grew lizards
      – scrub also showed life –
      but when his body made a long shadow
      stones were his company.

      Some said his purpose was
      'to explore the limits of human endurance'
      others that
      'his curiosity about life had gone'.
      Whatever – he should have taken only
      a machine into that death;
      what right to dehydrate a horse!

2.   After the rain the child
watched, inspected, in the sun,
drops swing along the clothes line,
stop, hold rainbows inside themselves,
clear, enlarge, hang ponderous,
then burst their birth on the ground,
again and again and again.

Shetland and Ponies

Light – when you come to this place –
light is falling from the sky
and the water is returning it;
the land, wrinkled and dark, a dead skin
that might crack open with no sound
and the bright water drain into that breathless dark,
lost like a single life in emptiness,
and not a tree to bless with its gentle growth,
but the bone of the world pressing through,
the stone face to which the human face returns.
Inhospitable but splendid – this North land
that tells the cosmic tale
of earth and sky and water.

Water – in the beginning a drop of water
and the light was in the water and there
each stone was shaped to be itself and none other,
each shell to be itself and none other,
each creature to be itself and none other,
peerie fish and crab and whale
seen and known and named,
yet unknown as the round of the sea.

I look into the glass that is water
and know I am a stranger to this place
I look into light upon light
and know it is not of me.
I look on to the waste of land.
I do not belong, but these

fourlegs make the spaces their own,
a backyard for their games,

a stamping ground for their romp
a prancing place for their pride.
They populate it with their warmth,
make jokes about the mountains –
this universe is their home.

Two Love Stories

For my daughter Marjorie

1. The old man
    is going into the dark valley
    that is his life now.
    Momentarily light falls,
    a shaft on his head and shoulders,
    as the girl meets him
    on the narrow path.

    She is a shadow to him
    as she skips off and on the stony way
    to avoid him, fumbling.

    She has come from the shore.
    She carries her bliss into the mountain.

2. On those waters a certain delicate
    pale flutter of blue silk
    under the moon
    has been known to mislead
    two into a sense of permanence.
    Pass then from the white shore
    crescent under the crescent moon
    to the lit harbour
    echoing the red and orange and green
    ship-lamps in the dark waters.
    But you will be deceived here too.

    Or is it that those years ago
    still stay awaiting recall
    when the echo of a horn will turn back
    to find the moment of making

    where there is neither time nor place.

Sonnet for St Francis, 1965

A fat squat man with a flat nose,
Dead brown eyes, heavy lidded, slow;
Stub fingered, puffy hands held in repose
On his knees, palms turned up as if to show
Nothing is concealed. He sits on the stair
Of a granite monument, himself a Buddha in stone:
In morning sunlight, wind, rain or cold he's there
Whistling a tuneless note from his throne
For his birds, pigeons that come fluttering
And tumbling about his rewarding hands,
Devouring, gorging – like a halo – circling
About his steady head. This man
Is their unknown god who blesses and will restore
Without a sermon – now and for evermore.

Philosopher

He gathers his days
as a child petals,
looks at them separately,
then together,
turns them over,
then leaves them alone

to watch them grow
as the hairs fall from
his head.

They will arrange themselves
and look at him
when his face has taken
to itself – silence.

Old Carlo

He carries the past in his shoulders.
Light caught him and the dust
that rose from the hooves and wheels
of the ox-cart weighted with
barrels with grapes for the pressing,
caught him in the white clearing as he moved
out of the shadow of the cypress
at the end of the road
on that October day – a late harvest.

The girl at his side, granddaughter,
is going to the new school in the old town
nearby. They teach science there,
physics and chemistry. In the stone
Mary the Mother above the door
and inside the Christ.

Second-Class Passenger

Leaving Florence, leaving the Annunciation,
Angelico's, top of the stone stair, San Marco,
leaving expectation, astonishment, veneration –
second class on a dry Italian day,

girl with a baby in the train.
Some time had passed between the events –
the paint drying on the wall,
a brown-eyed girl in the train.

Suddenly he tautens his neck,
makes to lift his head and you
with a single slight movement of arm,
encompassing, supporting, ease
him into sweet sleep.

Leaving Casa Macleod

Trespiano, Florence. A letter for Joseph.

Leaving you with permanence written
in the olive-leafed sky,
with the faces set
in the chemistry of paint
when Leonardo was young
and the oxen yoked to the dogma
of the stone pillars of Gropina,
whitened by the weathering sun,
a word to you, in the moment,
to fix things waiting for recognition.

When you put a house down here
in this kind of time, your walls
grow meaning from each stone,
each stone talking ten centuries,
or twenty: mentioning by the way,
the prehistory in the lizard
or the modern – Michelangelo.

Yesterday when Raphael was around
someone put a foot in the dust
at your garden's edge, firming the earth up
for the seedling olive.
This day, the tree's there still.

Fire and Earth

My attic window sights roof-topped
horizons with one gold autumn tree,
its branched candelabra lit
by quick-fire contained by earth's lid,
translated to finger tips of tree,
leaf trembling in a slight wind.
Somewhere within, the sap drives
upwards – like a flame held
in a lamp-glass drawn by the funnel –
chancing the setting bone of winter.
Somewhere a concealed bird sings.

O but this boldness is dashed,
put aside by the thin city mist,
whitening, flattening till tree
is delicate as a Chinese painting.
Without dimension, this world is quality;
like the air of a tune remembered
precisely, but long after singing.

Tree

Into a monotone sky a November tree
puts its black main-branch slimming to the top,
not vertical, but off course, the growth rhythm
one way, then subject to correction – the slow
dance of growth – the other, and each twig
starting from the tree turns and points upwards
into the blank day. All the leaves have dropped off,
the sky irresponsive and the air merely bleak,
yet each tip conveying a promise – made far below
in the black earth to the eye,
in its individual pointing upwards,
in its wayward yet controlled resilience –
of tomorrow. Tomorrow survival.
Tomorrow the sap will express itself,
in the first bud. God, if this fruit
is for this wood, why should that child
cry into her frightened night? Why
should men be computed as stones?
Tomorrow the idiot gun looks for another corpse.

Street Conversation

'In this wilderness, my friend – '
I said, standing on the kerb, corner
of Sauchiehall Street/Hope Street,
with the little football men returning
from their dream – Celtic, Rangers –
in the even light that swims
people and palaces (picture and bingo)
into their grey limbo. 'Watch,' he said,
'you don't trip on the stank.' I said,

'Outside the wolves howl in the red-green
amber winter lights.

               Old man, your face,
from the coal-face witnesses in favour of
the dust.'

'O.K. O.K. O.K.' he said.

Sketch of Poet

For Norman MacCaig

MacCaig angular in a wind-rainy day,
long, lithe striding to a shop;
at the lintel one step down halts;
large head swivels, toppling
eye over shoulder, stares – for what?
To pick the chemical sun from this gusty sky
to make fictions. He'll convince
parchment is split new stop-press,
crammed with the latest, liveliest,
nerve vibrating, lovely and tender
forms as enticing as girls,
as mature as malt,
so long only as the Word which is now
that spectacled old lady counter-bound,
exists. MacCaig enters shop.

Homage to Hugh MacDiarmid

(Age 75 on 11 August 1967)

After the rhetoric, the presentations,
the LL.D's, the public appearances,
the front;
         a few things worth noting.
At 8.30am
         in Princes St. Gardens
the lovers, having arrived from another country
and witnessed the Scott monument,
embraced.

'Meanwhile'
old man, you put a memorable foot
on the stone floor of your cottage
and waited for the day to catch up.
It was out there all right
breathing
     so you put it on paper
which you had done for fifty years odd.

What more's required of you
who put the breathing years in a pen.

After the Death of Martin Luther King

'Little children, it is for the last time.'

and each time it was.

He spoke with his body and tongue
for love.
God knows why in our bad times.

Credibility had long since gone
that the churches had something to do with the
Christ,
that the bombs dropped for humanity;
could not deceive any longer,
even the Americans.
But that he, such as he, could for
the last
     time
and again the
       last time
for love of, for the possibility of
healing, holding together,
possibility of resurrecting
the dead god of
       love,
Walk.

The lark sings Christ in the clear air.
O Memphis. O Jerusalem.

De Stael's Wall

At an exhibition in the Scottish National Gallery of Modern Art

1.   Fact. Registration.
It is finished – the wall,
rough-cast and established, apparently,
and the paint tactile and the mortar there;
wall made out of your too great exertion:
                         and then
the terrible knowledge as conclusion that every
stone holds, but. BUT shakes; but holds
(to save you, us from night).
Yet you achieve object, that, no more:
object achieved – wall. Finished
as you were in the fictive act –
to make order; order prevails
but the crevasse waits.

With this knowledge you operated without anaesthetic
on the nerve, on self and out of this willed
wall.

No more.

2.   In the afternoon
a girl walked on the bright grass
outside the gallery. High noon
for her.
    She did not witness your monument.

Laotian Peasant Shot

Seen on television war-report documentary

He ran in the living air,
exultation in his heels.

A gust of wind will erect
a twisting tower of dried leaves
that will collapse when
the breath is withdrawn.

He turned momentarily,
his eyes looking into his fear,
seeking himself.

When he fell the dust
hung in the air
like an empty container
of him.

Against a Wall

For all soldiers

They had clarity.

The simple news
that it was good
to be

no more
that was enough

fingers to touch
the blank wall
enough

till that moment
precise
as the trigger.

Down the years
we did not get
the message

but spent time
as trash.

Three Love Poems for my Wife

1.   TOUCH

and no sound
and no word spoken
and the window pane
grey in dwindling light
and no word spoken
but touch, your touch
upon my hand veined
by the changing years
that gave and took away
yet gave a touch
that took away
the years between
and brought to this grey day
the brightness we had seen
before the years had grown between.

2.   TOWER ON CLIFF TOP. Easter, 1968

When I took your hand, securing
you at the turn of the stone stair,
for the narrow step deepened by unknown
steps that climbed that dark,
(many generations in that dark
that split the day from day)
the sky broke blue above;
below the stone cube, the flat sea,
then in this place we knew
what we had known before
the years grew in us together,
yet never knew as here and now
in sudden glare and roaring airs,
as time had waited on this time
to know this in our broken day
when I took your hand.

3. LOVE IN AGE

Now that we have had our day, you
having carried, borne children,
been responsible through the wearing years,
in this moment and the next
and still the next as our love
spreads to tomorrow's horizon,
we talk a little before silence.

Let the young make up their love songs,
about which subject they are securely ignorant.
Let them look into eyes that mirror
themselves. Let them groan and ululate
their desire into a microphone. Let them
shout their proclamations over the tannoy
– a whisper is enough for us.

Visit in Winter

In the Highland hotel
the highland waiter
is waxed: in the off-season
when stags rut and their roaring
quivers the icicles from the eaves,
inside, in a ten foot tall bell jar
in rubbed morning coat,
napkin at the ready,
his brown eyes staring from his yellow
smooth skin, preserved, deferential,
he stands waiting in his improbable world

for the incredible August people
who kill birds and deer –
and not for need.
At least he can be verified,
visible in a tall bell jar.
Of the rest who found significance
in killing birds and deer,
we only heard tell.

Boarding House, Arran

The marmalade is thick
with Glasgow accents.
The cornflakes flute
with Freda's giggles.

Betty and Alec go
bounce bounce
in the
cold lemonade sea

that waited the round year,
as did the soft rain
for them, dripping
and yawning into their

honey moon-suckled night,
misted: in the morning
she collected
a smooth sea stone,

put it on the step
with love;
a stone is enough
with love.

Coach Tour and Locals

'Sunset-red rhododendrons –
to your left.' You look
with one neck. 'To your right
alone on the rock in the blue bay –
a solitary heron, the emblem
of Arran.' At the top of the pass,
'over there now hidden in the mist –
the white stag of Arran.'
With one head you look at nothing.

The little waves lap their feet
on the golden shore.
They look at nothing.

Success is to look
at nothing
be neither
yesterday nor tomorrow.

Yesterday the *Girl Jean*
running for tomorrow
with a fair catch
off Holy Isle,
struck an iron sea.
It took her and her crew
to the trash of the abyss.

Death was not their due.

A Pigeon's Feather[11]

by La Sainte Chapelle, Paris

These skies have never quite emptied
of angels.

Tack teeth smiling pin-tables,
nickel spinning miles of
battering fruit machines, op
pop, cliff-top in plush tip-ups,
wrapped goods – is o.k. for a
smart polish in a close neon night

but these skies have never quite emptied
of angels.

Out of that pale blue
Angelico in the Louvre
down by Sainte Chapelle
a white feather
                    floated.

Peace,
'nostra pace'
maybe
was somewhere around.

Camelia in the Snow

Life risks all in that perfection
in the blown bloom, pink
in crusty snow concealing earth.
The leaf is weighted with snow.
Small comfort the windbreak wall,
but flowers open to the winter sun.

Virtue from politics of survival,
seemliness. For black and Jew
strategies are necessity,
deceptions, lying necessities,
prostrations, bribes necessities.
We cherish our distorted faces,

that grimace guilt in eyes
of human hate, yet stare
with longing on that strange world
that blossoms in the snow,
growing where no life should
grow on this short winter day.

Look the Other Way

or you might see what the Pole and the Jew and the Black knew,
might discover that you were no other than he who
tortured and turned away or passed by on the other side, might
suffer the arc light of his mind whose sight you took away, whose
being destroyed; truth would destroy you – so look the other way.

Only he who with paint, stone, word, sound took out
of that Auschwitz the sad face, stricken brain, torment
for resurrection's sake (Christ's sake) for us today,
makes us whole; but you will look the other way.

The Word

1.   THE SEARCH

Now all these tunnellings in the soft dark
with the sand sifting and falling as fast as
you scooped it back with hands, fingers, nails
and you on all fours like a dog, panting till you
sweat drops dropping from your forehead onto
the sand, coagulating it, giving it a little hope
that the cavern would stay and you would enter
and find what you sought in that dark, what you, what
you had hoped for, but what?

or it was the ascent of the grey mountains and the dross
coming back at you sifting into your boots and you
coming down two for every three but pushing up and up
for you were the first ever on that waste – so you thought –
and you would find gleaming that hoped for bliss lying
in the ungrowing dust and the name traveller –
discoverer would shine from your forehead
as you came back from that farthest moon country

for you would bring back (ah Christ!) with all that toil,
carrying it in your hands, cupped carefully in case
it would spill or slip or fly up or vanish
and you staring at it so that it might not escape from
the beam of the mind, for over sixty years
this was your only discovery. Look and look
nor turn away or be stone (like Lot's wife) or
lose all in a twinkling (like Orpheus) all that
for which you had laboured and shrunken,
got wrinkled, bald, worn so that the lines
in your face were clefts; and this was it all,
this was what the distance of your short long life,
the running of life, the creeping and tugging, the
desperate heaving, the getting up in the morning,
the pissing in the bathroom, was –
to bring home the Word.

When they put the first man on the moon
and the dust rose about his five feet ten
he knew less than, less than that which I

had gathered, dug for, sought after with
the sweat of love, for I had worked
in the sterile deserts of brain. Sixty
years to find a, to find a, to cry out
Word.

2.   THE WORD IN THE HIGH RISE FLATS, EASTERHOUSE

At Easterhouse she was pinnacled in the tinkling skies
high, so high – as she did her nails in the pink morning –
she saw onto the Lochs and the Lomonds in her pin-up head
and heard the sweet guitars of Balloch as they swung
from the golden shore into the blue ice-cream loch
with their honeys for bliss. In these skies,
while the patch, sixteen storeys away screamed with
the blood of councillors and bus drivers and what not,
he planted his seed in her soil.

As smooth, as bright as chromium, all her days glittered
in her nine months, sunshine, and not a doubt on the horizon
for FLAT 2007a, sixteen floors up (one down, the intellectual
roamed his Borroughs fackwords and borwards – and no outcome)
but *their* word was flesh, and straight, flash-Bingo!
seven garden dwarfs, two cocktail cabinets and color telly
were his – him straight from her plastic womb up there –
all his, who would never smell the sour smell of the
breeding earth.

And the product of her parturition, from the dumps
and dunnies, grew teeth, razors, chains, flick-knives,
to comfort his solitary confinement in the flesh.
And the dust rose from the long shitten dry yard
about his eyes, he hugging the smoke from the fagdowps
about him, 'case he might know himself from her,
him from him, her from him, might know self, know
he was one, one alone in the breathing night; so –
Ya! Bass!

3.   THE WORD

A hand up to touch on an airy day a small blue butterfly,
not knowing why, nor where, nor distance, here, there,
nor word to know what, but look sensing the moment of now,

when no time is, the hand up to touch, clutch
nothing, not knowing space, but in space he is,
space-belonging before time claims his coming.

Belonging? Being – his being is when she only,
smoothing the pram cover, moving at an angle
to give food, shelter, covering; when she is bending
as an arc of sky round world's curve,
bends over – her warm shadow is day to him –
she is Word to him, day and night word.

Our night – the myths creep to their holes.
The sky is a hole. Freud dug his garden
and the serpent became worm, and the worm was earth.
Humus, in the beginning a garden,
in the end magma.
In the beginning and end, the Word.

Winter Bird

And every winter on the stone sill
supported on two wires that splay till
they become four springy toes at rest;
the red burns upon the breast,

bringing into the ordinary dying light
into my constructed code
your being that stains the snow
and will not let our guilt go.

Quixote in a Windmill

He saw it hoisting itself from salt marshes
into his trembling sky. It stood
on the edge of water-meadows turning
to marram grass turning to sand only
and then shallow pale sea.

He looked at the broken webs
that cracked but did not move.
Once this castle was his when
the wind bawled about, the sails
whirled in the turmoil of his mind;

racketing, squealing, grinding, they became
his madness: he watched his brain lifted
to the brazen sky, thrown down on stones –
he was King for a howling winter
till the soft Spring came and flowers.

Autobiography

For years
a schoolmaster looked over my right shoulder
in case my punctuation went wrong.

For years
a minister looked over my left shoulder
in case I committed a moral solecism.

They've gone.
Now I watch the sparrows in the green grass.
'Lechers!'

Reflection at Sixty

Thunder knocks about the house,
tries doors and windows.
Night. I listen in bed.

Somewhere around
there's a birth going on
that concerns me.

At Bridlington Spa
my wax moustachioed purple uncle
used to sway in the salted breeze.

'Give it up,' he said,
'All this bother about meaning.
Douse lights and out.'

Transplant

'Christ!' said the surgeon, 'It's not there.' Though why
he should have expected it, considering
my heart has been in my mouth for years.
So there they were scouting around,
pulling up the tripes, chasing along the long gut,
digging the bowels, hugging the liver,
freaking out the lungs, inspecting the duodenum –
and nothing in sight. Zero hour and the trumpets
sounding. 'Christ!' said the surgeon, still doing
his nut on the wrong tack. The trouble was
semantics. Shouldn't he have known
– O Lamp of Licht –
Christus Victus, Christus Victor,
Kyrie Eleison – the water of Babylon.

Somewhere along the computerised line an omission.
Feedback. Reprogram: LLLLLLLLLLLLLLLLLLLLLLL
libliblibliblibliblibliblibliblibliblibliblibli
'Got it' he said. LIBERAL STUDIES.

Municipal Comment

12.50am

Writing after midnight,
a slow fire going out,
cold settling in;

reminders and questions.
Now we've got moon dust in containers
there can be no more lunatics.
Remove that word from the vocabulary,

and think of Town Councils,
impeccable in their honesty,
undeviating in their purposes,
beautiful in their opacity.

'It is essential to keep things circulating,
a road to keep four wheels circulating.'
They circulate.

'It is imperative to build twenty storeys vertical.'
They build twenty storeys vertical.

I pay my tribute (exacted)
and regret the loss of a word.

Houses

Suddenly our house went up in the air.
The slates, rafters, chimneypots, masonry
burst out like a gust of starlings
and stopped 30 feet up.
They then decided to come down again.

That was 1941.
I believed my mother was inside.

In Edinburgh houses come down.
Without giving notice the cement balcony

of a council tenement left its assigned
position
and made a new map on the pavement.

Our house is different; it is very old,
it creaks a bit in the wind,
is water-tight now and then,
comfortable for mice with good runways:
it should do my time.

Home

1.   KEY

Two hands it takes to turn in the lock
and every night squealing, juddering till
it's home, locking them out, us in,
the dark out, the stream in the dark
that goes through the city carrying
what's jettisoned from life.

Two red candles on the mahogany table.
The table reflects our faces; pale
transparent we present ourselves
to ourselves at the agreed age, mature.
But who is that old man on a stick
who looks at me from the mahogany?

2.   THE BIG ROOM

In our house I light the fire in the big room
with paper, sticks and matches. It heats a small area.
I sit close, holding out my hands, spreading fingers
to the flames; they become transparent, the bones
shadows beneath the skin. The fire throws shadows
on empty walls – cold out there.

Black and yellow out there. The big-eyed children
stare. Some are at the breast, some by the mothers,
seated row on row on the floor. No room elsewhere.
Our house is built of stone to shut out –

I look into the fire. The mothers hush their hunger,
whispers rising from the floor. Today

I fed the bird with Christ's blood on its breast.
He came to the sill out of blank December,
stayed for bread, now claims this territory his,
interrogates my eye, bawls out the sparrows,
allows none other (Qui s'excuse, s'accuse).
The children's breathing comes about me cold.

My faults domestic; failure to keep the fire
to shut up house; confess to having swept
crumbs under the carpet – matters of little consequence.
Dinner is served at eight. On the mahogany
the knives are table knives, red candles, goblets –
domestic rites, no sacrifice intended.

Perhaps one day they will go away,
run into their yellow sunshine.
In the church I shall take a collection,
'for the poor brown people far away.'
The walls sweat. 'Rising damp', they say.
Don't mistake me. We never had the torturer here.

3.   THE BEDROOM

Here her apple-green dream in high summer.
Cornucopia. Lawn curtains lifted and fell.
From her virgin bed, in oes, in spangles,
in to-fro runs mingling lights and shadows, water
mirrors itself on the ceiling, a shimmer
from the slipping river running by the green plot,
her garden below. Bird voices of children.
'I am on my swing and swing so high
that the bright sky brushes my eyes.'
And over the wall where the stream
is glass the swan placed to be seen.
Untouched by tomorrow or yesterday
tea will be served on the lawn
and afterwards, chocolate creams.

4. THE STUDY

I secrete myself between two commas with
Jonson, B., Marlowe, C., Shakespeare, W., Webster.
My banker uncle said: 'Poetry gets you nowhere.
Give it up. Besides . . .' Byron fornicated,
Shelley ran starkers in a drawing room,
Even Wordsworth once got a girl with child but
'that was in another country, and besides
the wench is dead'. 'The small fly goes to't.'

'Birth, copulation, death. Birth, copulation, death.'
'*O lente, lente, currite noctis equi.*'
Shut the book. Too many indignities.
The Bank must be protected from life.

5. THE NURSERY

To write my first word
I was set at my little table.
There would have been no difficulty
but that I felt the ogre's head
move under my feet. It threatened
to roll out from under, creating
acute adult embarrassment, a trauma.
(One has no wish to alienate,
stretch the credibility gap at age eight.)
What they cannot understand is that the gaoler,
clicking her needles, counting the stitches,
at the ready to drop one when the next head
falls, put there for company, (they say.)
adds to the overcrowding. I have already
to support in this place the woodcutter,
charcoal burner, witch and potions
serpent and tree, one bird of prey,
the dwarf, his ape, weasel and hog,
a gold eyed frog, one mandrake root,
one buried heart, one red rose with dew,
one glass mountain with princess,
one with no name. The conditions
for attention to the word were becoming
unfavourable. Correction – fortunately
it was butcher meat under my feet,

slippery under the texture of the sack.
When she complained the light was going
I was grateful for her momentary inattention.
(The floorboards creaked. The river was high.)
She said: 'Last night the shadow of a man
crossed the window, but say nothing of that.'
As if – but the blood was oozing
through the sack on to the soles of my feet,
dripping on to the floor, silently; mercifully
as long as the condition was private to me,
– she could have her sex – it was possible
I might still deliver the goods, write
down the word for which they waited
patiently and calmly in their place
of order and disbelief. For them
the river runs by the garden wall,
the rose bush is pruned in the spring,
the green swing untied for me.
For them the silver knives lie on the table,
the candles, red napkin, the goblet,
each in its appointed place and when
the clock chimes from the mantelpiece
when I have put on the white paper
their word – they say – I shall play,
but the beast kicks in the sack.
What did they do to the wound under my feet?
The wind rumbles about the corners of the house.
The little match girl in the weak light
warms her hands at the last match.
She glows in the garden like a tree
by the sick rose and the water.

Witch Ball and Old Fisherman

for Archie Turnbull

This green world was his drowned eye
suspended in the small, shut window
through which he saw the sea pounding
at a safe distance. The old man
was now removed from death.
His daughter handed round the tea,
served in brown-flowered china cups,
a wedding present forty years ago.
I shake hands with her at the step.
He looks at me through the green ball
in the window, watches me fluctuate,
submerged in a swell with the garden flowers.
I am in the salt waste he voyaged daily
for food and without a thought.
A boat's siren sounds from the harbour.
A lorry rasps gear, in a cloud of dust.

Making a Poem

Some days words come at the run
like boys for supper.
Clean and firm
they present themselves
alert and at attention.
These days are worth waiting for.

Perspectives: Poems 1970–1986

Prologue Visions

Old Man and Sea

Nightfall – was it still out there?

The rusty, white iron gate trembled
as it opened to the path to the sea
down by the ramblers, unseen,
no scent, for the salt had taken over.
With all my fearing childhood in it
I hear it growling in the dark. Ahead
from where the marram grass meets sand,
between me and the slapping water – a figure:
he stands square-shouldered staring
into that nothing.
    How many mornings
when the silvered horizon promised,
giving hope for that day
or when the mist stood impenetrable,
or when the sky burst and the sea met it,
I thought, he waited, thought I knew him,
might approach, touch him, claim him for kin,
he who stood his ground for us all,
but there is no reckoning in this matter.
Square-shouldered I stood looking into that nothing.

Between

Always as we lifted our eyes
from that dust which told us of our deaths
it was there waving, juicy, yet wavering
through waves of heat: and we were forever
approaching it, and forever watering
our spirits so that we did not know
we were little other than dry bones.
Now, though we had died then, having
many times reached that place where
our spirits and eyes told us green
grass grew: though scientists and doctors
had simple final explanations that
what we saw we merely imagined, did so
for the sake of sustaining our mortal bodies

as if they were immortal, still
with wilful obstinacy, stupidity, we believed,
totally convinced there was a place for us
where the lark above sang in her blue sky,
and below meadows sweet with running water.

Then they set the computers on us to produce
the final evidence that we were predictably computed,
and that the final figures were on our brows.
There was no escaping the verdict.
We drew a circle in the sand.
Within it we, the last of the believers in
that seeming state – between – would
perish, die, not for lack of sustenance,
but through the now accepted rationale
that all could be accounted by the tool
that plotted the graph of our being,
reducing, with absolute precision, to formulae
the excited tremblings of what we called spirit.

Then one observed:
'The circle itself is an abstraction.'

In the Beginning

The Visitor finds Eden in Australia

Suddenly they addressed themselves to him.

The kookaburra gave its heartless laugh
for him. 'Curra-wa, curra-wong', sang
the pied currawong. Twenty sulphur cockatoos
cursed above from the white gum's branch.
Bush parrots, rosellas, king parrots, even
a lyre bird, presented their credentials.
A coiled yellow-black snake uncoiled.
The curiosities of nature were on display.
Trees grew out of dust, lifting themselves
light-green and airy into the steady blue.
The sun hoisted itself into the northern sky.

She walked among the falling gold in late
autumn sun, and not a stitch on her,
ran, jumped under the tumbling fall
that sparkled from its source in desert.
The koala, of course, clung to his
god-like presence, adoring as ever
those who assumed worship as their due.

When he turned his back did
the scenario, so carefully scripted,
collapse? Did the scene-shifters
go about their business removing
the flimsy structures, spitting
on raw hands, the show being over,
or is all as it was after his darkness
fell, waiting for another?

   . . . And in Scotland

He had come this way before
when the little fish of childhood,
inches long only, and quicksilver,
but pink beneath the dorsal fin,
moved with superb locomotion,
and the green crab, awkward, scuttled
its side-wise motion under a rock,
when the beaches offered see-through
fan shells, the size of his pinkie nail
and fabulous whorled shells that echoed
with hushings vast unknowable oceans.
'Write it doon,' said the whorled shell
into his lug. 'Pit it doon for your Da.'
Write it down for mother, for father,
for all the forked kind, the big heads
with eyes that read. 'Scrieve it,
scrieve it!' scraiched the gulls.
'As Duns Scotus said,' said the Prof.
'objects may possess individualities
peculiar to themselves. This thisness,
haecceitas, should be a central interest
in your papers. Evidences are expected
as witness to your conclusions.'

The Witness

Witness to what? Each page continued
to make its proposals to him that signs
should be put on it, that these
might be picked up by unknown eyes –
an assumption that the deadly rains
had not already destroyed all witnesses.
Certainly there was an impression of continuity:
a cockatoo squawked across the leaden sky,
a snake disturbed the waters that rose
above the floorboards of the room.
But no planes, no comforting sound
of a combustion engine. Of that solace,
the accompaniment to the routine engagements
which had made civilisation possible,
nothing. No receiver of signs, then no
necessity. Yet perhaps as that last bird
sped between the boughs uttering harsh cries,
as the snake's body looped and unlooped
in muddy waters, there was the last requirement
to find that impossible speech which sang
of the creation that was.
                              In the dark
gathering in that upper room, he looked out
at the swaying, cracking branches – sound:
sight – possibly a twinkle in the leaves:
then in the perceiver light in the eyes.
The sweet word rolled from the tongue:
'Light. Light. Light.'

Chestnut Tree – June 1970[12]

This year the candles came late.
Waiting for June they burned in the sun.
At night they lit the moon that lit
the destroyed graves of the children of Peru.

Candles – do you burn with hate or love
or with nothing at all? The priests
lit candles for the dead of Peru,
walking into the ruined night for love.

The candles erect on the plangent leafage,
dance a ritual dance in the Scottish wind.
They incite the children to tumble,
to ride their bicycles without hands,

to ridicule an old man passing by,
to swing on the plunging branches in the wind.
The children shout for joy.
They disappear into the body of the tree.

At night the tree is a torch.
Its bare branches are ash.
A bird flies into the sky.

G. B.'s Sea Symphony

The conductor with his white carnation,
one hand on the steel rail of the rostrum,
the other, baton raised to the blue sky,
conducts the waves. They roll towards him,
endlessly pushing their white sibilance,
while the ocean gathers its symphonic mass.

We watched from our cracking deck chairs,
listening to the swelling adagio. At allegro
ripples pizzicatoed at the black coat tails.
He swings into a crescendo, ripping the sky
with a stroke. From their backsides on dry land
seat-holders glimpse the frenetic point of his up-beat.

The prom-strolling dainties, yellow-teethed old men,
groovy, geared groups, holiday haymakers on the blistered
beach, saw nothing, heard nothing, while the North Sea
sent its blue word over our conductor. In a trough
we saw the head turn, the circus white-wash face
with the jelly lips, the gaga stare. No encores.

You read this score once. The beach attendant stacks
the chairs. Five pence a time to watch the breakers
whiten in the sun. Tomorrow the next of kin mounts
the rostrum, raises his baton; they are the lemming
kind, ridiculous, mad: belief swims in their heads
that the earth makes music for them, for us.

From the Shoreline

Moon Men

Back from the moon
on the white officered
ship, the moon rocket captain
shook hands with the top people,
known by their gold braid.

In the sea village of Cairnbulg
John shook hands with
the fisherman, Jeems Buchan,
who had got back from
the moon-controlled Yarmouth fishing,

while south having taken time off
to inspect the *Codex Siniaticus*
in the British Museum.

Jeems Buchan put his foot
on the grass at his doorstep
took thirty steps to the sea
for seventy years.

Gilbert, his son,
stood on the slippery deck too.
The conditions made for
adaptation to novelty.

He was expert in the use
of radar and the lot,
became a naval lieutenant,
returned from the war to fish.

John stayed at the croft
that looked to the sea
kept a bull.
Jeems kept a cat.

Little puss, little puss,
hunting a sparrow,
looking for salt fish
between earth smell and sea smell.

Little puss, little puss,
as you pad between
brine and bull,
earth trembles, sea shudders.

In the night
John hears the bull thump
at the post.
Jeems the sea's roar.

In the night
a gale couped John's rick,
took Jeems' yawl clean
from beach to grass.

No fishing
for three days,
then flat calm
and a low mist.

The white lifted
from the sea's face.
An arctic tern
exploded the silver.

Jeems said,
'We're for off.'

As specified he collected
rocks and moondust,
carried out the complicated
measurements and operations.
noted the effects of asteroids,
meteorites, cometary materials,
set up instruments, checked gauges,
returned (as programmed) to the machine,
arrived, having accomplished
marvels of precision, celebrated,
at the ordained place and time,
home on the unknowable earth.

Sit by me, little puss,
sit by me, little cat,
who looks for the remains
of fish.

Look wisely and run from
the trembling sea.

On the white plain
he lifts his limbs in slow motion
moving towards the edge
of the disc that recedes
at the pace of his steps.

The occasion lacks gravity
as he rolls on lunar business.
With full military honours,
at attention, vertical, he plants
The Stars and Stripes to canned music.

Home, a dog barked in the night.
In the Spring the crocuses came again.

And Did Those Feet . . .

Black in the morning sun, Sunday boots
athwart swinging shoulders, feet pad white
across three miles of sand, upright men
bound for the kirk, who swung off Kinnaird
for fish. Necessity, custom, and in their heads
Christ calling his disciples, sinners who'd
boozed last night, a few taken illicit sex,
most held to their known purpose for life,
resolved, drowned in tears, howled at
by evangelist Jock Troup, washed by him
in the blood of the lamb. Christ have mercy!
Monday – John Gatt, who'd done it all,
locked to the deck in his balancing act,
has no ministers, nor booze, nor grace in his mind.

Sea Men

1.
'God in the wave!' Joe bawled as it rose
and shut out the sky. How! How? –
when the swing took the boat to his death.
No words in that waste. Black she foundered.
The Lily, her curt moment stretched out in
wind-wail, sea-moan and a wrecked moon.

The cliff house waits in the long dark;
nothing given away about the life,
that must have been, must be there
still in the dark that moved
while the wind blurted about
the stone corners that stood on stone.
Inside the place awaiting return
her world stops, blazes and cries.

2.
Spewed out of the sea we crawled in the dark.
Hung nets enmeshed, creosote in cans, tarred
ropes coiled – we smelled our way like animals.
At dawn we struggled to the door and saw
the long, low light greying the horizon.
Salt tingled our eyes to life. Our soft
bodies felt again the rocks that bled us.

Set this down in a hand that shakes.
Each knowledge requires respect –
Smell tar, creosote, wood and salt air.

Death of an Old, Fat Seaman

Round man on the empty crude oil drum
With your back to your mentor ocean,
Twelve miles in your tipsy yawl you'd come
To settle for, sing for, line for your portion
Of fish, for thirty years supported
The flaunting seas with a legend –
O rotund porpoise! 'Indestructible', reported,
Fixed in space without a wrinkle to portend
Age. As you rat-a-tat fat hands on your drum,
Squat Buddha, inscrutable to tourists, dumb,
You're hauled heavenwards, strung up at the turn
Of tide, caught in the bare light of a winter sun,
And float in the air like your simple tune.
At night I see you bellying the full moon.

Catch

For Alexander Scott, poet,
on his return from Greece,
loaded

You, Alex, went to the Aegean,
came home with a shining shot,
clean, unmarked fish.

I shot my nets thirty miles
East of North off Kinnaird,
came home with spents,

the rest torn bellies.
The dogs had got them.
Too late in the season.

That's what legends do,
purify the seas.
They're in short supply here.

Oil Men

In memory of William Burns, R.S.A., (1921–72)

The silver darlings had gone black,
rotting at the gills, the spermatazoa
on the wane; propulsion of energy
from below the North Sea bed,
a shot in the arm for a dying society.
Looking with green eyes
into the now recorded depth
I spotted the new squid
whose dirt's consumed by
homunculi-on-wheels hellbent,
while I would plunge headlong
into another unknown.

William Burns took other soundings.
A Glasgow man, practical, he
piloted a plane in the war, then flew
one to help him see the face of Scotland
abstract; settled for Aberdeen,
Art Lecturer, gave up to paint only.
To see better he flew over north-east
ports, studied spatulate piers,
geometric blocks that would concede nothing,
nor were asked by his art. He put
in the rectangle of his canvases
trawler keels, rusted plates, seams caulked
with red-lead, boat rudders that nudged,
awkward propellers, tarred planks, ropes,
white-washed wall, bollards – his canvas
a scrap-heap for forms that had long resisted
salt air and the gale. Stumpy kirk towers,
fishermen's block houses at odds with weather
came together in blobs and stabs. Lumps of paint
patched his square – his sea-town picture,
his sea-town spotted from his plane,
gone over with meticulous eye to bring
back the life that lies in wait in objects
men used to combat sea, and in the spaces
between artefact, sea and air. He made sorties,
piloted his plane on the edge of mind to see.

All over again I hear through his paint the boom
of the foghorn that howled in my child-nights.
Then it juddered the window frames set in granite.
My childhood rises from his cold look.
I heave in a mist. The story begins again,
hauling itself in dark and silver.

                              Keel over – he keeled
when once more he went on survey into his last mist.
He left his findings for the rabid few, who
(against all the blank minds taking their gain)
hold to that other.

The Return

Salt on the lips and the sea unseen,
unheard; the air swinging in the head,
sheer light breaking in a shuttered room,
a torrent, the senses alerted at each
moment – this freshness remembered.

Our kind's productivity deal takes over –
the dead gull's wings weighted with oil,
plastic cleansols rule the waves,
the waves returning faeces to the shore,

Hidden in a dip in sand dunes, the wind
beaten back, sea-sound a murmur, a shelter,
where the sand loses itself in soil,
thyme and forget-me-not. Our cold
summer sun makes this a place again.

Honeysuckle

Honeysuckle grew at the back door
of the house sheltered from the salt
wind by the granite wall. Girls came
to kiss there by the washing green
and the honeysuckle blossoming
while the sky was falling into night.

Under an impeccable noon sky
father left by the front door,
shoes shining, moustache bristling,
navy suit without a spot,
to do business, with a view to
profit, to keep the house upright.

At the back door the stars
reeled about in a purple sky,
drunk on honeysuckle dew.
Into a night of small noises,
voices one to another – lovers.
The back door squeaks shut.

Sea-town Genesis

This orb – a sea moon –
was the brazen gong
that hurled our young
to love on the sandhills
that faced the sea:
on the lea side
the wind sifts the sand
between the iron railings
that enclose the flat
tombs of their fathers.

Under the Moon

The flowers that fringed the waves
waylaid, sucked his white body
in a wild wash, cut by sharp rocks.
This was the death of a swimmer,
a boy, in November, moonlit.
Lovers walking on the sands did not know
his time had run out, theirs being
fulfilled in hushing sound,
turning gently the shells on the beach.
She picked up a fan, a pink shell,
held it transparent before the moon.
'Love, put it in your pocket for me.'
He put her in his pocket. The waves
whisper in her shell ear, 'Love.'

Two Together

The moon ripens in their eyes
on the silk of water. As two walk
in themselves as if in each other
the terrible entry is being written.
The sea gives up its dead.
They lie on black beaches
in the squalor of our night and day.

Alpha and Omega

Out of the inchoate
walking simply on moonlit sands
she came with a formal look

she to him　　he to her
her to him　　he to she

she composes herself placing
a lock of hair to flow
from neck to breast, turning
from him to sea.

On the beach short arm vertical
his fist squeezes an apple dry.
Its tears run into the shitten sea.

Gulls and Fulmar Petrels

Voracious it tore to rags skin and
flesh, herring in the barrel, fed
till its belly ballooned, but weighted,
trapped, so, constrained by wood, hinges
of flapping wings could not operate.
Gulls lumber in the air anyway,
while fulmars, stiff-winged, plane,
flip from cliff edge tidy, or rise
in an air-stream effortless –
a-poise, the Platonic bird itself,
the bright bird belonging to all
the wild airs, not submitting, but riding
all ease and gain in storm, high
or low shadowing frothing breakers,
or down skimming wave trough –
a delicate ghost, a spirit soundless,
an implication of an absolute
wrested from (denied by) the destined dark.

Words on Beach

Went to a stony beach to look for agates,
found none but came back with bags of words,
agates, chrysophates, pure crystals, carnelian,
as many as I wanted and much easier to carry;
took them home and began to polish them,
cracks and impurities in them too.

G.B. on the Rocks

The facts of time sit on my balding head,
while the permutations of water affront the rock,
water day and night on it. Speculation will not
alter its longevity, nor mine. I consult my drying skin.
Curious that in these circumstances we sing,
while fate drowns the precious young,
trips up old friends, damages the innocent.

The Stones of Iona and Columba

They define themselves rarely
in the walls of the abbey, each
inviting attention as it shapes
in the mind, pink, grey, blue.

So through the glass of sea
on the white bed each stone,
insisting on its difference, presents
itself for the first time,

surprising us with the shock of light
and with the knowledge that it,
like God, has never been seen,
but with love a little known.

The sea pitches. The boat is thrown
on the stony beach. The cliffs echo.
A thousand years ago or more he
picked up green translucent pebbles.

Still they are strange to us. It is enough
the stones stay.

Boy and Cod's Head

The grammar lesson. *Macbeth* as specimen.
'There is no speculation in those eyes.'
The line jumps from the page: gets lost.
Lines are for peerie fish, podlies, codlins.
Macbeth – a play. I play football. Sand blows
through the grasses of the football pitch
by the sea, the cemetery on the other side.
The fog settles down – sea smell, sea sound.
On the spit of sand, bleached white, a skull,
rabbit's, sand sifting through the cavities,
the bone structure a palace for life once,
where the dance began, the leap, the twist,
the scuttle to be safe, now safe in sea's cycle
with thin fan shells, buckies, whorls,
and the pink dried back shuffled off the crab.
At my feet a cod's head chopped off
its fish body, cast overboard, spewed out
with guts, entrails, blood, reject of man
and sea, a violation of nature.
'There is no speculation in those eyes.'

The Desert and Other Moralities

On the Roads

Little children
walk
in their bones
on the roads

Hump backed
wi her creel
the auld wife cried:
'Herrin. Herrin!'

An the skipper said
tae the auld wife:
'There's ower mony herrin
in the warld. Pit them

back til the ocean.'
And she did.
'Ower mony herrin
in the watter.

There's nae eneuch bellies
in the warld tae feed.
Gae back tae the sea,
Ye auld wife.'

She cam oot the sea
and she went back
intil't cryin:
'Herrin. Herrin!

An the deid herrin floatit
on the watter.
Says the man that kens:
'Stop huntin thae herrin.

There's nae eneuch herrin
in a' the seas
tae feed thae folk
on the roads.'

Dust in a dry wind.
Hard in soft mouths.

The Desert

For Hugh MacDiarmid

I

POSTCARD
(Photo of Yasar Arafat, Nasser and King Hussein)

Nice photo – all smiles but
the middle one's dead. The one
on the right, the King – he swore never
to shake the hand of him on the left;
he's the guerilla, commando, freedom-fighter,
and *he* never, never, never to cease from
fighting till the King was dead.
They shake hands on it – all's peace –
as you were before the fighting started,
because the one in the middle said, 'You'd better.'
which is fine, but not for those between.
The freedom-fighters weren't to blame
for hitting what they didn't mean to.
The King's men weren't to blame being under orders
from the King to shoot the guerillas who were
potting them. Bad luck. And now
when the King says he will never never
shake hands with the guerilla again
and the freedom-fighter says never
till the King is shot dead,
who will be the smiler to say:
'Call it off, boys, till next time.'

The location for this set-up is
the cradle of faith, the birthplace of love.

II
You know how in the desert
there was nothing to eat for the chosen people
till it fell from God's sky,
white and momentary as snow –
a violation of nature, a disruption
of the organic personality of the desert
where death was its order. All very well
for the politician, one thing one day
another the next, that's diplomacy,

organisation. He promises manna
which once consumed ceases to exist,
whereas the desert is rock, unconsolidated
but consistent to its own laws,
making credible the idea of finality,
and to disturb this was for God to
become a politician, for a moment the
creator less than the creation, nor
of it like the politician, who has
always a reason for doing that which
is palpably wrong to all, but him,
like arms for South Africa,
and at the same time he is a
Professor of the Christian Faith.
This is the nature of the politician.
He sloughs one skin at night and
puts on another in the morning.
These curious manipulations
are embarrassing to human observers,
but never to the Politician who
is protected from self-perception
and from observing the reactions
of human beings. There remains
the question – will it ever be possible
to bring together the human observer
and the Politician?

III
HIMMLER IS MY BROTHER

Once I took him for that
everything else followed naturally – the trains
trundling their loads to the gas chambers,
the station masters, guards, signal-men,
assistant signal-men at the points,
the villagers acknowledging the trains on their way,
accepting their processions as the final solution,
the trains singing to the rails:
'Himmler is my brother. Himmler is my brother.'

It is the solution of the desert,
of the mushroom that the Americans
first grew in the desert, of the

corrupting of the lungs, of the tree
that no longer breathes seed,
of the children of Vietnam
that no longer breathe
who ate of the tree of the
knowledge of evil. 'Himmler
is my brother, is my brother.'

In another country the sea lay on the right hand
and the clover flowered on the other.
The children ran after the small blue butterflies
that rose onto the air from the clover,
breathing its scent into their nostrils.
The mother called the children home
in the evening, in the morning the bell
called them to the village school.
Peewits flopped in the air.
Cows rubbed their hairy backs on posts.
In the school the children learned words
so that they could know of the desert far away
that would one day be their desert.

IV
'Sir,' I said, 'it is impossible,' and left.
The CO's instruction was to find three wells in
a thousand miles of Lybyan desert.
He had it 'on authority', he said,
'the Romans used them.' And in view of what
was going to happen when war broke out –
it was 1929 – it was essential to locate them:
'it might save the lives of British soldiers.'
I had a school friend posted near
El Alamein in charge of a camel corps.
He said: 'Yes, you can find the wells.
Go to the escarpment; get on a knoll;'
and he named it – the name was Egyptian
and doesn't stick with me – 'take your men
there and wait. In three weeks you'll know.'
So six men in turn, from a wooden tower
on top of a knoll from dawn to dark
watched the rim of the desert,
and no-one came. 'We'll stay for three
more days,' I said. On the second day

there was a smudge at the horizon.
It moved. They came – a dozen or so families,
men, women, children, camels, mules, goats,
hens, – and their gear. They were on their round.
It would end and begin again where they
had sown barley seed. They would cut
the plants that would be ready now with their
sickles, then sow more, then go on their way,
on their round, into the sun, over the sand
to another well to sow more. Their time was the height
of the sun and the length of their shadows;
the boundary of their country, the moving horizon.
When I could guess at their number
through glasses – sixty or so, not counting
the children, the huddle turned away, became
a snake, going east. I got into the transport,
an Austin Seven, and hared after them. They
stopped, when I came up to them in my cloud
of dust, as if under orders. Their faces
showed no interest. It was like being looked at
by a picture – the women behind their yashmaks,
all old faced, the men, scraggy, stripped of flesh,
with faces like scored cliffs, big feet
for the desert, large lean hands; the children,
black eyed, keeping the animals still,
one, his legs like sticks, tethered to a jackal
dog. There were infants, one being given suck.
Then the leader came, made in joints, to judge
by his walk, propelling himself with a bleached
staff, taller than himself. 'What did I want?'
They could not halt here. They must be
at the well by dark. He stood apart.
They watched him, silent. Round him,
round them, the desert. I watched them go,
diminish, move unhurried as if each movement,
every awkward jolt of the camels, whinny of mule,
lagging footstep of a child, had been predetermined,
was repeating what had been done in this place,
this emptiness, a thousand times before.
At the horizon's bound I made for them,
came upon them gathering together.
The leader raised an arm high in gesture –
'Come.' It was the right time and place.

They gathered their whiteness about them
in the white blaze. Empty kettles and pots
clanked as the mules halted.
Eddies of sand stirred about their dirty
clothing as they rested. The sand
was a burning glass that threw the heat
back at their flesh and bones as they sat.
The boy with the dog went into himself;
waving date palms swung in his head,
bursting clouds sailed in his sky, waters
rushed between his green banks.
Then the camels sighed, men moaned
as they took themselves to their feet
for the way again, to leave behind
the smell of life that had gathered into
their circle, made it a habitation, a home,
a boundary of life, where life was insupportable.
'And there was nothing hid from the heat.'
I took bearings and noted on the map,
with protractor and compasses, the location.
I looked back to where they had made a place,
which was now again the desert. I looked forward
and could see no way.

Before night-fall they went through
the Breasts of the Virgin. Her stone chin
jutted above two sandstone rocks, moulded
by the wear of wind and sand, that narrowed
the way out of the round and so into a wadi
and down the dry bed – and beyond it to one side,
the well. They squatted, made fires; for
the first time children screamed, men shouted,
the dog barked, women gossiped, the camels
lowered themselves to the ground for unloading.
The water was fresh, not brackish. It was green
nearby, but little growth. No palms.
This water had watered the animals and people
of the Bedouins before the Romans came.
They had known the way to the well before Christ.
The well and the way to the well, the rocks
that would not move, and signs I could not see,
talked to the boy with the dog, imprinted a language
to carry the round of the course that was the year,

that was the measure of the desert, that was
his country, his home: and the language
would have travelled to his children and to
their children, but for what could not have been foreseen.

When Mussolini took over the Italian Empire
he asserted the boundaries on the map.
In the desert there are no boundaries,
only the shifting horizon. When the tribe
came to the Breasts of the Virgin,
they saw jackboots that said:
'This is the boundary. Go back.'
They turned, knowing there was no
way back, no direction, no time that way,
– you cannot turn back time –
no return to a source, no water.
A British plane saw a straggle of
men, women, children, with animals –
and one behind on the desert.
The tribe died.

The Little Match Girl

There is
      a moment when
in our city Novembers
(this day) when

the river swings its spate against the
garden wall; debris plugs gutters, the mains
flood; just then
when an old man in a darkening room
looking through the transparent flesh held
against the flames – then

she stands amongst the brown leaves
in the back-garden, with the river bank
just beyond where the washing hangs,
pale with large eyes and straight thin hair
falling on her shoulders, aged
childhood into womanhood –

she is the little match girl.
One after another as dark falls
she lights her matches; they glimmer
momentarily, then drop silently
into the dark grass – one after
one after one after –

      It is the regulation
scene of neglect, the condemnation
of the capitalists of the nineteenth century
who profited by starving the people
who worked for them, then charitably
starting Christmas charities. Those poor
died so that the Great British Empire and the Good
Queen could show the World how Great was Britain.

We do it differently.
In the last match she is aflame.
She burns at my back-door in Vietnam
or wherever.

Politics

I
For a time it was
'Gentlemen.'
Later
'Friends.'
Then after the change of regime
'Comrades.'

In any case the processed
applause – 'Small crowd applauding'
Disk 75289X – was the same for each.

II
In Florence
they have a nice economy.
On Saint Antony's day they display
banners for the saint. The next
day being the first of May
the reverse side is shown –
Hammer and Sickle.

III
In Ireland they do it differently,
Fratricide.

Theological Pieces

I
I dig the garden for a worm
for a hook.
'Uncle,' said the worm to me,
'do not put me on the hook
or I shall remind you ever after
that you have been on one
since they kicked you out of Eden.'

II
The coal mine of my mind
is sufferable
when others acknowledge the condition
as theirs; less so when officials
of the mysteries
insist they have a searchlight.

III
'O.K.' said the Master of the Mysteries,
'but who is going to shed light, if I don't.
Try an expert in defoliation –
a geneticist.'

'One day,' said the geneticist,
'I shall come up with a man who
will see through the coal face
and round the world
till he gets a back view of himself.'

IV
My face is a cliff face
scarred.
A hole in the middle opens.
'God.'

I eat another apple.

Worm

I

Earth movers who
move it by
passing it through their strip,
leaving it at their other end,
their ten hearts beating as one.

This action
predetermined the rose
that still sheds blood
on this December day.

II

The adoration of the rose
is the adoration of the worm.
Praise Freud
who gave another Eden.

III

Love still is
when two are one.
This I know
for so
I was begun.

IV

No serpent.
No Eden.

Angels' Wings or Whatever

When I was very young, a sprightly angular boy,
they were everywhere, but especially under my feet,
lifting me up – I went loping through the air,
(as all the Stars, football and female, do now)
in slow motion – so I was captain of the football team.
They called me to the rooftops and I climbed
in the dizzy air. It whisked around my big ears,
my nostrils gathered the sea-smell from far-away waters;
my eyes collected the bright beach and the rocking boats
in the little harbour at one go. I sat on the golden roof top.

> 'What is the laddie daein there?
> Why does he no come doon?'
> I'd gie him a skelp on the bare
> backside gin he'd been my loon.'

And not a wing in sight. I'm old. They're back.
Black winged and bloody mouthed they buzz finance.
The blind businessman takes them for fruit,
the generals for friendly warheads,
the scientist developments of the genetic code,
the New Left for the resurrection of Karl Marx,
the New Right for an English Christ to destroy black power.
Would God the skies were empty again!

Moralities

> Used to steal turnips,
> swedes, with blue tops,
> long light-green shaws.
> This was allowed.
>
> Once – they grew in open fields –
> greenpeas, two thin boys
> with arse-holed shorts,
> stole. Immoral.

Angels

For fear they were not there I
could not look at the spring-green trees.
For fear they were not hanging
from the catkinned branches
I looked away.

I said to myself:
'All this unexplained energy,
all these hanging delicacies
and the slow vegetable trunk,
isn't that enough?
You don't need angels.'

Now they hurl themselves
about the sky,
shout doom.
I can't look up for fear.

Folk

Single Ticket – Edinburgh/Bennachie

'I made up ma face to gang oot
but I made up my mind to stay in,'
she said. Help! Page a psychiatrist,
or a poet or a fiction writer or an architect,
or a Scottish stockbroker. 'Well, hen,' says
the stockbroker, 'what ye need is an entrepreneur.
He can go between, and I'm the very boy for that.'
A passing Professor of Linguistics remarked
there was a distinction to be made between
the use of 'made up' with respect to the face
and the mind. The fiction writer said:
'Who done it? It's a whodunit. Who made up
her mind? Who was in the house at the time?
It had green shutters and there was a father.'
The mathematician said it was an 'unresolved equation'.
The architect said: 'It is a question of room space.'
The poet said nothing. The lecturer in linguistics
returned to say the problem was linguistic.
Was she Scottish? Was she English? She was
the split product of a split nation.
'Mass schizophrenia,' said the psychiatrist,
'incurable, terminal.' ('The Scottish antisyzygy,'
murmured the poet, but nobody heard.) 'And
there is no dialogue between the personae!'
'An fa's speakin,' says Ma breengin in
fae ooter space jist as the conversash
is gettin hetted up. 'Naebody's speakin
tae naebody. An neen o' ye is gyan tae hae onything
tae dee with my dochter. She's comin stracht back
tae the back o' Bennachie, wi her Ma, faur there's
nae personality nor linguistic problems,
faur Natur rins the burnie tae the sea
wi'oot let or hindrance, faur naebody
maks up their faces, an aabody's
made up their minds lang syne.'

An Interview with Rembrandt

It was, of course, an impertinence to expect
even an admission. He was, as we believed,
in the Seventh Heaven. Some said he had
identified with God, but that was putting it
a bit high. He was not to be seen, but
might be heard if he cared to utter.
Decidedly he would respond to a question.
'Rembrandt Harmenszoon van Rijn', I said,
(the informality of the Christian name only
was out of the question in heaven) 'it is
your immense charity that shines from
the faces of the people you honoured in paint.
What was your inspiration?' A voice said:
'They peyed me for't but nae weel eneuch.
Hardly the cost o the paint an canvas.'
'But' said I – we were off course – 'all
these years these images on the walls
have spoken of humanity. Saskia – '
'Saskia' the voice muttered. 'Ah Saskia!'
'And the woman in bed pushing back the curtain.'
'Her? Weel, there was a spare bit canvas.
She was a dacent body – dacent to me.
An the licht was on her. Licht'
he said, 'let there be licht.'

There was a pause. I could hear heavy breathing.
I thought he might have been a little more revealing.

Rembrandt in Age

Self-portrait in the National Gallery of Scotland

He kent, as thae een lookt at his
oot o the dark he made in yon picter,
he lookt on a man, himsel, as on
a stane dish, or leaf faa'in in winter,
that calm was his strang souch.
But in that dark twa wee lichts,
een that shone like lit windaes,
an in that hoose muckle business,
words an kindnesses atween folk.
Aa that steir in Rembrandt's heid,
or, as some wud say, in's verra saul.

Woman Pitten Back Night

A Woman in Bed *by Rembrandt*
(National Gallery of Scotland)

Risin on ae elbuck frae the box bed
wi rumpelt claes on't, she lifts,
on the back o' her foreairm, the fall
an lets the licht luik in, syne stops
so's to catch up wi a new day.
He sees her, thinkin, 'Wife – nae bonny,
but sonsy, strang,' syne luiks again,
an what he sees he pits in paint.

Noo a'body gangin by yon woman
in the picter, maun stop an luik again,
for yon was first-licht he saw
on her brow. He made her
as love traivelt thru's ee til 's haun
an intae thae merks on a bit canvas.

The Nightwatch

The Nightwatch *by Rembrandt*
(Rijksmuseum, Amsterdam)

Dab hauns at the money gem, he thocht.
'Mind the step. Maister, as ye gang ben.'
They cam in tae get pentit, bleat wi pride,
padded burghers – ('burghers,' did ye say?
Weel, let it staun at that the whiles.')
Rembrandt gets on wi the wark. Ootside
they're for hame, ilk ane dressed
tae the nines, siller buckles on their shuin,
ruffs whiter than a swan's down feathers.
An say they felt – as pure as snaw,
til hame, an bed, sarks aff, breeks aff.
They weemen's nae doot the stuff they're o'.
They haud their gab forbye, but Rembrandt kens.
Ilk ane for what he was, he kens, nae foozlin
him, but he kent tae they micht be waur,
as weel as better. Sae he pentit them,
nae naukit tae the bane – was he no a man
himsel – nae starkers, but *sympatico*,
but nae eneuch tae please his maisters.
Na, na, this was 'letting the side down.
It wasn't cricket. Wasn't the man being paid
good rates for the job?'

This day three hunder year
sin syne, or mair, they glower, or peek, or luik
oot o' their dark, or raither Rembrandt's dark.
wi licht i' their ee. Was that no eneuch
to be alive as that, while we lie doon
nicht by nicht in oor benichted sauls:
nae sun, nae stars abune, nor mune,
encapsulate in concrete, or airn, or
God kens whit, waitin for the nameless
finish.

Would that Rembrandt or God would luik
wi seein ee intil oor ee that yet can tak
an gie a little licht – the Licht itsel, mebbe.

A Hind's Daughter

by Sir James Guthrie
(National Gallery of Scotland)

Nae kailyard here! Nae clarty dubs.
Nae feeling looks, nae heivenly thochts abune,
Nae gentlin a'athing owre wi saps.
Nae dribblin at the chaps and doffin caps
Or gien a nod tae God to say, 'It's me.'
But here cabbages sproot.
A quine wi a sharp blade in her haun
stauns in a field at Cockburnspath
richt as she did.

The Vegetable Stall

by W. Y. Macgregor (National Gallery of Scotland)

'Stall?' Na, 'sta' – a wuiden bench wi a wa ahint. For Sale –
tatties, neeps, ingans, leeks, carrots, kail, rhubarb –
the hail jing-bang o' needfu products o' yirth, in paint
as doon-richt as a Clyde boat-builder's haimmer, an that's
whaur Macgregor belanged. He says tae his freens and learners:
'Hack the subject oot, as you were usin an aix.'
Kokoshka cam by, lookit lang an lang at Macgregor's picter.
Hardly possible, he thocht and said: 'To think this picter
was made afore I was born.' In auchteen-eighty fower
Macgregor brocht thae objects and paint thegither,
louped the gap, ilk stroke to mak tatties, neeps, rhubarb,
themsels in truth, that's new an auld, on that canvas
that stares at his, aye yet, this day, as time stude still
frae then till noo. O tae hae sic sicht thru hand an brain
tae stop the universe in'ts track, an see't for what it is!

Chopin at 10 Warriston Crescent – 1848

for Alicja Danuta Fiderkiewcz – pianist – 1974

I

Thunder and silver – the air trembling.

We came upstairs with the invalid Chopin
climbing the turning stairs, Everest without oxygen,
then taking all his heartache into his music,
blood on the stones of Warsaw, memories
of his defiant country and its terrible history,
he put them down, inarticulate marks on a white sheet.

You, a girl, found his heart in your fingers.
The red deepens in the roses,
the dark rages outside the panes.
The refugees are taking to the roads, old guns fire;
despair rattled the bones of the frail man
at the piano, who was about you in that room.
'Remember,' he said, 'not a dying man – '
Dry leaves dance in the street,
in the salons mazurkas and polonaises,
the banners of liberty on the snow, scatter,
are taken into the future in a small room
in another country.

II

It wis the cold that got ye,
and yon twisty stairs; you sclimmin
them like yer hert tae burst.
Everest wi-oot oxygen tae you –
sync at the tap, the piano
an ootside leaves gan heilster-gowdie.
Ye were fair connach'd,
or sae we thocht, but some pooch
in yer hert had virr that ettled
tae win oot, an did, in your fingers
till thon hoose rocked in your thunner.
The siller leddies, hauns in their laps,
gied naething awa: the gents
lookt like stookies (an mebbe were)
but you soon't oot a' rooms an ha's

an ower a' watters tae Europe
an across the plains wi snaw
whaur merched the Poles, an
puir folk wi a' their warldly gear
upon the roads – thae refugees,
then an noo.

                  An so's your music
then an noo in a lassie's fingers,
makin sic steir, the air tremmlin,
speakin your leid, your folk's leid,
an oors, a' wha bide haudin
tae themselves, that benmaist thing
that dwalls, waitin for the kinlin
till the spark loups at the hert.
Then a' the trash o' the warld's
forgot, a' the riff-raff wi naethin
i their heids but the neist kick
o' the ba that lang syne's burst.

'Tak hert' says your sang. The snaw
tummles on Scotland and you're awa.
'Maks nae odds. I'm in that sang
that soon't yestreen, the-day,
an will dae the-morn an a'.'

Ae Nicht Fire-Bleeze

In Memoriam Barbara Hepworth (1903–76),
who died in a fire in her home in Cornwall

Night. Nicht. Wha's?
The nicht was hers, her

that strung strings athwart the rock
tae mak dumb mass gie sang.
Then, thonder, ae nicht fire-bleeze,
a lowe on the warld's rim, a sun
that ate the doors o' the wast
ridin the watters, takin
till its end humanity.

Them that kens that kens a'.
Was't no eneuch tae sign her mortality
in veins ridin the skin, blear een,
crevasses dug in her broo, an wyte,
gien her ae last chance tae gawk
at winter tree an mak it bleeze
wi Spring in'ts form, her takin't
frae natur tae gie it tae oor natur,
so's when we lookt the flooers lookt
oot anew. She took stane o' a' kind,
marble – black, gree, Parian, white
alabaster, ironstane, pink Ancaster
stane; the wuids – red-wuid, rose-wuid,
sycamore, African black-wuid, beech-wuid
an a' ither tae uncover in theirselves
purity in essence. But she's nae here tae
tell the tale in daith is life, in lumpen licht.

But noo I look on the Burnet rose,
a composition in white marble,
ilk petal a marvel o' precision.
Touch – ilkane as saft as flesh,
an scentit sweet an shairp.
The flooers float in air,
the roots trail in aneath the rock,
traivellin the bank tae get a haud
O' yon yird that's Scotland,
tae souk watter an iron mell't
thegither, an syne stravaig
the sap o' life alang thae veins
till oot intae the peelie-wally sun
that we've brewed up in Scotland
tae mak dee for the real thing.

Noo, when she in Cornwall
coost the clean shape o' things
in truth, was't no for his tae,
for aabody, as when yon rose
gies sheen tae oor pit-mirk,
that tae's for her an his an a'.

300 Days Rain

I stood at the window
and watched it dripping down,
dropping down the window pane.
Across the street – the School.
Holidays – hurrah! And the rain rained
on the school and on the grey street.
Said to my Dad: 'How long?'
'Wind's in the East.' He said,
'Three days at least.' Three
hundred days I stood. Stood.
And the school was not washed away.
And the boats did not sail in the street.
And our headmaster was not drowned.
And there was no call for Noah.
There was nothing. 'Nowt' but drops
dropping on the pane till one o'clock,
when Doughy, the big man with the big
moustache at the burroo who paid
the workless workers their dough,
came swinging up the street, swinging
his rolled umbrella up the street
and singing! Swaying full sail
to our sharp-right corner. Would he
bloody his bald head with the
black bowler hat on the black
railings as, half-seas over, he
swung out? 'He'll do it,' said
my dad. 'Shorten sail!
Hold hard! List to port!'
Like a feather in a gale,
true as a glass of whisky
he rounds the point – and gone.
And gone my bliss, and the three
hundred days of my seventh birthday
go on and on and on . . .

At H. C. Anderson's Hus – Odense

For Kai Greiber

So, before the little mermaid swam
into him, before the little match girl
and the vain emperor, before the snow queen
and the constant tin soldier, the nightingale,
and the dog with eyes as large as teacups,
the dream that dreamed up the painted houses,
red-coated postmen, top-hatted chimney sweeps,
cobbled streets, yellow lamps and the dark,
the fairy tale was written into the stones
that waited for the poor boy to grow
to tell the tales that knocked on doors
at nights like drums that drummed, 'All's well!'

Karen, Age 1

She knows
the flower in the grass
beckons her.

It does not move.
Its yellow eye
looks straight to heaven.

She stares
at the day's eye,
would pick it up.

Towering, toppling,
her body equivocates,
wavering

till it stands erect again
still swaying as if
straining in a great wind.

Then flops on her bottom
on the green grass.
Daisy stares to heaven.

She ponders her long day.
The earth presents its fruit
to her immense grasp.

A dog barks far off
in his other world.

Child and Tree in Autumn

Last night's rains ran the river mute
giving no sound to the morning's sun.
The fir plantation bends to the flowing hill
down which a straggle of copper beeches take
their doused fires to the water's edge.
From the bank the haws' red suns flare;
drenched rowans shake their fruits above.
Herds with swaying udders fulfil
the autumn day. Painted by a child
a house sits square in the middle.
Upstairs a face at a small pane peeks,
travels the canvas as if it might tear open,
the precarious moment swallowed in dark.

Good Morning

Feet squelch on a brown Monday morning
that hasn't had time to put its face on.
Gutters run. A bus washes the corner with mud.
A child, nose flattened against the glass,
sees the world new. In his heaving ship
churned-up slush is a wake of creaming waves.
A woman in a green hat, stuttering on high heels,
is Spring. I am in his looking glass and hear
hooves' thump of lambs' dance on thin turf.
It pushes them up into the blowing sky.
As the boat moves out smooth beyond the cliff head
my long drowned innocence rises and breathes again.
Those aboard have no truck with water,
which has killed their generations, but to hunt fish.

It is nothing but a use that will exercise cruelty
as wanton as malformation. 'Good morning!'
Is this then a lie that the absurd face at the pane
conveys, seeing miracles where there are none,
but that the eyes are wonders.

Lament for the Passing of the Hissing of the Steam Trains

For Jennifer

Now the grandfathers tell
their grandchildren,
'There was no thing like the hiss
of a steam train.

Wisps of white
swam over wheatfields,
encircled briar roses,
fled into the blue,
went boldly over Russian snows.
When they cut down the Cherry Orchard
steam trains were heard.

Now that steam trains are gone
we should give up hissing
for joy
as do the ripe cornfields
as we passed in summer winds,
as does the bell heather in light
air trembling as we passed by the glen,
as do the soft small waves
on the shingle beach under a quiet moon.'

never, never, never, never.
will they see, hear the great
gonged trains go so again.

Lost Boy – Liverpool Street Station 1918

The legs bandaged in khaki, big boots
clobbering the ground. Bound trunks
of limbs going up into suffocating nothing.
Escape. The hand of the father held my fist
tight, till suddenly it rose away on important
business. Cigar. I smelt it. An unseen thread
pulled me through the labyrinth, and I was there
at *The Rocket*, at the gleaming brass body,
the bright tall chimney pointing skyward.
'Please put a penny in *The Rocket*.'
Wheels go round. Some day it will move out
of its glass prison, will chortle
and steam, throwing up white plume.

Through a sweet countryside wisps of white
swam over wheatfields. My steam train
picked its way through strawberry patches,
heading hard for our cold north suns,
entered dark glens, trembling the bell heather,
shouted a little as the sea hove in sight,
ran by it as the small waves beat their own
time on the shingle beaches under the full moon
that had filled our mouths with silver
bellied herring for as long as my black-bearded
grandfather had roared: 'Praise the Lord!'
to welcome the boats to port. 'Toot', said the Lord
as we slid between the sea and clover to the stone
platform grunting and grinding, pshawing to a halt.
Our white plume rose on its column and spread – home.

'You were lost, you understand, lost.' Lost?
Why shake me so? I did not kick, bite, scream.
Better that we do. The boy dreams.
We have our nightmares.

Old Man and Child

seen through a window pane

Bone of my bone, old bones,
rags and bones you are: through
frosted glass under a yellowed
sun he stoops to a yellow crocus,
will do so till earth slips from him,
and he marooned on the island of self.

Dance boy, dance on the bright grass.
It throws you high to the sun.
Dance, dance, you are light to my day.
You throw no shadow over my way.

Leaf Falls for Old Man

Holding his eyes to the hardening
earth, the inconsequential moment
becoming dust as it fell from blue,
scarlet and sere, the leaf, rocking,
turning a slow spiral in the still air,
its veins dull red riding the skin,
he witnessed his joy becoming him.

This fall persuades there is no sere,
no flint, but calls to winter bird
and beast and man to bed soft down.

North Coast Cherries
For Elizabeth

All around
salt in the wind
a mile from the sea
salt on the tongue.

Against the wall
that faced south
sweet red cherries
enjoyed by stealing boys.

When I think of you
through many winters
cherries ripen
in the sun.

January Haiku
For Elizabeth

She sits in
Arizona sun
snow on low
juniper and dry grass.

Do not disturb
this moment. Wind
blows, dust rises.
Time takes away space.

Sit still in this
moment elected
by who knows what.
Now dew beads grass.

Sonnet on my Wife's Birthday

All the love I have will not take her years away:
All the knowledge given not grant her time release,
Yet one day less impoverishes this great feast
That grew when we together went our way,
Hurrying to meet our newly planted day,
That barely showed above the stony ground
Of our North-East, whose grudging air beat down
The rare freedom that becomes when two are one.
So, when every loss is gain, as every colour, brown
Or red or tarnished yellow in our life's spectrum,
Shows itself, why should we protest too much
Against the silent pace that makes in us such
Speed, for we have learned to plant our love so strong
Our children's children now take up the song.

Old Snapshot

The camera's shutter clicked. He'd caught
her for himself alone, he thought,
standing slim among the marguerites
against a sunny, summer wall with apples
on it. He put her in his pocket book in 1932.

The sepia mellows, seems to tell more true,
not just that moment long ago; collects
the happiness that walked through shady lanes
and by St Machar's towers at crook of Don
and through the Auld Toun's clattering streets,
bypassing the Bishop founder's tomb, to King's,
to sit amongst old words long dried on the page,
mountains of them, beautiful and boring,
wise and absurd – and still the moment breathes,
disturbs their dust.
                        Another place, another time,
from which she still looks out from that mute world
amongst the flowers, grown now most delicate.
And all the air of this dull day is changed.
Landscapes shout new with spring. Seas glitter
in their calm, and I, this breathing animal,
own such sweet strangeness as no words will do.

Elizabeth Polishing an Agate

My love, you are pulled into a stone.
The skies run into night,
The stone stars are there.
In this lost momentary world
you treasure stone under your hand,
seek out what is most unlike,
smoothing stone like glass
till its fixed hair lines,
finer than Leonardo's line,
mirror stone's permanence.
There are no seasons in a stone.
Lode star it draws you,
you giving your brief warmth
to stone.
Gone, it stays cold.

A New Perspective

Aborigine with Tax Form

'. . . even though you are reared in a city out there, you're liable to feel when the hot wind blows, that the city would, in fact, be blown away and that you would be faced with this kind of interminable, extraordinary bush landscape which goes on for ever.'

Sydney Nolan

He was in the taxation office in Sydney
(God knows why) – and with a tax form,
a white paper (A4) with words printed
on it and question marks. He was
one brown, gnarled, grizzled, almighty
question mark under the electric light
of the concrete edifice: his category –
'black' he insisted. Place of residence –
'Australia.' Home – 'Australia.' Still
nothing on paper, his fist on the page.
Outside, the hard sun was on his fellows.
They sat on their hunkers on the flat
stone paving. Tower-blocks soared skywards.
Steel, glass, the synthetic scape took over.
Not quite; in Sydney the sea is not to be
denied. Sun beams its flash into high-rise
executive suites: it gets a peek at the stock-exchange:
it interrupts art lovers in the gallery of N S W.
Insurance blocks in George Street are the less secure
for its glance. Its smell settles on roof-top
restaurants. Seagulls thieve food at the Opera House.
Budgies flutter their colours. Pelicans, even,
float around in city airs. Sea, air-borne dwellers,
disturb the city abstract, ask questions
that will not stay in the parameters of paper.
Inside HQ taxation, Sydney, they play taped
soft western country muzak to assuage Australian
tax-payers' nerves. Inside he is still there.
Head down, the crumpled features, visible just,
the broad nostrils, till an upward glance,
flickering eyelids betray brown eyes –
staring at the black marks on white paper –
see nothing. For him nothing is there.
He is become a no-person, an astronaut
who has lost touch with his ship,
becoming vibrations on a scanner,
will be so until he puts foot on earth,

his earth which grew this dark earth man,
who named Australia's birds as they cried:
kookaburra, kookaburra raucous, currawong,
currawong – a song, a morning song in flight,
wurra-wurra, cooee-coee – koel calls,
bock-bock-oo, bock-bock-oo gobbles wompoo
pigeon, oom-oom-oom woops pigeon, jabiru
– silent hunter, brolga – trumpets brolga:
ear echoes to calls' bounds and re-bounds off
cliff-face, rocks, silver-barked trees,
waters boom, sky will black with thunder.
The red fire-god raves through the bush:
all is ultimate, so this man-Adam lights his
home places alive with sounds – Andamooka,
Thunda, Goorajoo, Nooka Warra, Croajingalong,
Wagga Wagga, Woolanmarroo, Booroorban, Boort,
Boonoo Boonoo, Murrumbidgee, Murrburrah. 'Ha!'
But *he* calls out for the newborn world.
He calls out with the astonishment of the child.
'Oo!' 'Aa!' cries the child as the stars were
new made for her, for him, for the whole being
child is, 'Kangaroo!' shouts child in man,
and the original is made. It thumps, pounds,
leaps, is at one with no man's land.
'Warringin' – wild dog, the teeth are bared
in the word: dried grit, sharp stone in the word,
and the land stretches its bone in an eternity
of distance: no living land, but suns, dawn to dark,
will not blaze away the guana still as rock
at its rock. From Dream Time (altjira bugari),
the founding drama of sky and earth, the beings
of the kingdom, all creatures – man being one – came.
From then a spiny ant-eater, with sensing snout,
moves out from stone to seek its food, survives
as *he* survives in this, the land he shares with gods
– the animals, so he acknowledges them the inheritors
of that first great stroke. They honoured him
by their presence – all in the rite of life, the dance
and song of life. The water in the water-hole
is the water of life for all life. Here in drought
the animals drink their fill, and no spear
will pierce their hides. This is the Secret Place,
forbid to hunter, place of mystery, of renewal

of flesh and spirit life, of being. Bird, beast
and the desert tree whose root drives down as deep
as branch's tip points skywards, draw from the source
of life-song. The bond between all kind stayed desert,
till the white man came with his guns
and Jesus. Jesus, black Jesus, was in the eyes
of the children. The white man did not see Jesus
in the eyes of the children. He saw black savages
who blocked the way of progress. In the name of progress
and Christian civilisation they increased productivity.
The commodity, sugar, was in demand. They imported
Kanakas blacks from the Solomons, efficient hands.
The Kanakas yearned for their home ways and meat.
On Sundays the white men went to church.
After church they gave guns to their workers,
who killed for meat the people of the land,
who when they stood, stood as tall cedars,
when they moved were clouds walking,
when they ran it was as the antelopes,
every syllable of their being uttering
the messages from the generations back,
in the movements of legs and arms,
the gestures of hands and fingers,
the planting of feet on the ground,
the rhythm of torso and thighs and breathing.
Christ wept in the eyes of the children.
In Sydney in the taxation office, the official,
pale, slim lady in a grey suit with handkerchief
peeping in a red pyramid from her breast pocket,
looked kindly on the native. 'The Aranda tribe,
I think?' she said: yes, but in Aranda speech
there is no word for tribe. The bond is speech.
The Katitja, Iliaura, Unmattiera are bound
in intimacy and ritual by Aranda speech.
Now he is seeing his journeys, the sand, spinifex –
roots, grubs, lizards for food: the long walk
in the night air, in daytime sand and rock burn.

Day dawns: it is home: crickets chirp insistent
from river grass: birds shout: streams talk:
voices echo from the gum trees' shiny bark:
he is made anew. Brothers, sisters, mother,
father would welcome him – but no-one. None.

Kangaroo and emu fall to the white man's gun.
Sweet meadow grass turns to dust. Where was song
a new desert. 'You need assistance,' she said.
'An aroma of animal and earth,' she felt,
'hung about the office after he had gone.'
She saw them in a huddle shambling on the street.
They smiled, giggled, their shoulders shook:
laughter, outrageous as a kookaburra, explodes.

Astronomer

Now going into the presumed ends of the universe
he listens to the faint illiterate stars.
He has placed his warm heart on stone faces
he does not know, in undefined wildernesses
wandering to chart what has happened
beyond belief aeons ago.

He is a number to a number to
a computer to a number.
He is an equation waiting
for an equation, an equation
which is Astronomer.

In the interstices of time and space
a sparrow fell. Teach us,
the bleak discoverers, how
to witness to time and space
and to the blood of a sparrow.

Is James? Is Janey there?

Why do they do it to us – these phone voices,
thinned down like Giacometti sculptures
to next to nothing? 'Is Jamie there?'
it seems to say – plaintive, female – and I,
'No. Who?' Is Janey there or was it someone
else? Who speaks. She won't tell. Why not?
Exist – does she? Conned. I am connected with

space only. I am a chance component in an
electronic module formulated to utter: 'Is
James, is Janey there?' Where? Not here – where?
Who? Is there a candidate for being, a something
that may become the instant another says – 'Yes.'
'No!' I deny existence to the given. Given:
James, Jamie, Janey – electronically composed.
Answer the question on one side of the page.
Translate into persons. The question presupposes
an examinee. This machine is a word-maker.
James, Jamie, Janey do not materialise.
Sad toned they swim in their universe
like astronauts, who have lost touch
with their ship, who have become vibrations
on a scanner, will be so, till he put
a foot on earth. 'City of the dead'
said Scott at Pompeii. But they had walked
with friends, lit fires, embraced at night,
talked face to face to become themselves.

The Psychiatrist to his Love

*(Experiments at Edinburgh University have shown
that if a person is deprived of dreams at night,
hallucinations will follow during the day)*

'Ah, my sweet,' said the psychiatrist
to his love, 'now that I can
deprive you of your dreams at night,
you will have them open-eyed in the daytime.'

He took the sweet smelling pines
that stood by her white sea,
the leopard, the lamb and the serpent,
and the white ass from her dream, the
lily cloud that sheltered him from the
sun in her night, the moon-lit beaches
where she walked in her advertisement,
the furbelows and flounces,
the mutton-chop sleeves and the
embroidered petticoat from her sleep
and put them in the box for morning.

During the day he gave them all
back to her. 'Sour milk,' she said,
a wounded old woman. 'Put them back
into the dark,' she said.

Man is not a Fish

For Mark Horner, swimmer

He is a fish as the water falls from him
as he encloses himself in that fluent glass
to be nothing but one thing as starry suns
fly to his lips in the lapping water.
In the faint green, angel fish flit,
transparencies: an absurd crab scuttles
on the floor: no world for speculators,
but being. This is not the element
for the forked mammal imitative
of fish perfection, weighted by his thinking
machine.
          What god is propitiated as the body
in a bow-bend stretches in a split second, striking
the hard film, yet being received softly into a depth.

All our knowledge is nothing before that incoherence.
All our words burst as bubbles at a surface.

The Runner

This race I run alone.
Hands dangling, limbs loose, waiting
the moment of entry eye catches eye
of daisy left of dirt track on a green plain.
I run. I lift the green grass into myself.
Breathing lengthens and pulls with
calf muscles, thigh muscles. Change
stride: go lope for distance. Strain.
The drummer heart demurs. Slacken.
I find self in the iris of the daisy,
contained by white petals in the calyx vest.

Now it carries mind. What was
ground rooted now a yellow sun
to be held, to hold mind's eye.
Wings beat in the brain, I stay,
take earth into sky. Into the
meadows of my poverty the sun
steps. I am earth and light.
Clouds move under my feet.

Sing

Written for my students in wheelchairs
at a poetry class, St Andrews College,
North Carolina

Curious that
in our circumstances
amongst the hurt
we sing.

To sing we tear
the veil of reason
to make a vessel
for love.

See, it spills over
nor shall any catch
such drops who will not
know the blind god.

Poetry Circle in a Square Room

In the centre of the room
a squat man in a bulgy suit
has put his cap under the chair
upside down into which he coils
a snake like a scarf.
He knows it is not a snake.

It might be convenient if it were
for his nostrils sense the
woman enter, seat herself behind
in the far corner. As she crosses
her legs under the red silk
dressing gown there is the
silk worm sound in his ear.

She contemplates the grey,
horn-rimmed girl with the flat
shoes (perhaps she can write)
sitting on the outermost edge,
angular in the front row.
She opens a new note-book.

Snow falls. Snow falls.
A black cat is at the window.
The lecturer will not let
the poem in, dismisses
its green eyes to the darkness.
The black cat leaps from the snow,
stares at the pane,
silent, asserting nothing:
leap – a felt movement,

effortlessly creating the
moment that is one thing,
her poise, less precarious,
she acknowledges, perhaps,
our world inside. The snow,
a blank page, acknowledges
her delicate tread, her imprint
of a moon-lit traverse.

Precise shadow, you are
a presence to be shut out.
Admitted, your intolerable
completeness would destroy us.

Winter Matter

We have visitors who would prefer
not to be known, squeaking and prattling
along corridors. I leave a little
provender for them – cheese.
No traps, no such unkindness.

These are country people seeking
the warmth of our home, have come
into the city homeless refugees
from blasted fields, wrecked
by secret agents. At night

I come downstairs, barefoot,
a cold foot on linoleum. One
is there, or is it another,
less welcome. Big brother is
throwing his boozy weight about.

The house shudders. These are not
the eyes that bead gently in the gloom.
These bite the hand that feeds,
lodgers, who come to kill, eat flesh.
Wood rots, stone cracks, fire eats.

That's the way it is these days.
Everything gets out of hand.
No place for decency.

January Visitors

We were visited by bullfinches
this Monday morning. Immediately
we were in an exclusion zone: barriers
were set up: the chemical destructs
we had absorbed from laden airs
floated from us: the neuroses,
the nagging knowledge that our governors
were insane power seekers, the desperations,
vanished. Subtly these formal presences –
neat fitted black caps, deep-pink down chests –
persuaded us into their limbo.
Each green blade that pushed through snow,
each crumb set on the stone window sill,
presented itself in that new light of day.
(Yet through the pane the shadowed human face
that could not know that other place
where no time is, but every moment now.)
They sang no songs.
Doubtless they had no concern for us.
Doubtless they came for a meal.
Doubtless it was fortuitous they chose
our backyard for their landfall,
for that momentary enlightenment: gone
in a flirt of wings.

*Gitanjali**

On being asked for a poem 'for India'

Outside my window
leaves from the sycamore
blow about my patch.
Over the low stone wall
a muddied path, a tangle
of tussock grass, weeds,
the Water of Leith,
no holy river Ganges,
no Lethe, a mud brown,
swollen burn charging
in spate, bearing away

one thigh boot, two oil drums,
one armchair – the stuffing
milked by the water, a stained
white cloth unwinding slowly –
city detritus heading fast
for the Forth and the North Sea.
My stare telescopes on the brown,
but who is this large-eyed,
black-haired girl – child,
brown as of the water,
in a long robe to thin ankles,
suddenly grown in my garden?
She stands in the welter.
Her grave eyes look at me,
Motionless she holds a ball.
It has landed on my plot.
I smile at her. 'It is not
important,' but she
stands silent. She looks
upon the ball as if she
held in her hand her world
of pain and laughter.
She is from India.
'Your name?' I ask.
She does not answer, does not
look from the silvered ball,
bright with intermingled colours
flowing, unending in the round.
Slowly she lifts her eyes to mine.
'Gitanjali.' I do not catch the word.
'Gitanjali,' her name. 'Song Offering.'

Gitanjali was the name of Tagore's first published book of poems, which name was
given to the Indian poet who died in her seventeenth year.

At the Villa dei Misteri, Pompeii

The sacred Agape! A young girl bears a dish
with votive ornaments. Silenus plays his lyre.
A dancing satyr gapes. The Bacchante kneels,
touching a drape that conceals the object:
of love, fecundity and peace. Another
in formal dance, dances in exultation.
Prelude to the act the bride initiate
waits upon the mystery of the ceremony.
Dionysus, god of generation and the dead,
communicator of the loving cup, she waits
the phallus unveiled; her bowed flesh
accepts the whip. Now she stands poised
on this two thousand year old wall
that did not crumble when Vesuvius roared,
where still the lustration of the fire glows
from red walls about the dancers that shed
their pallid light.
                      A party of German tourists
take over the room, packed, back to back,
face to face, backs to walls. Their guide
recites the facts, the facts, the facts.
Knowledge and incomprehension spread;
a rash on bland faces. 'Tomorrow Athens!'

O goddess Athene! O Neptune, Poseidon. Venus, Aphrodite!
Diana – presider over glittering oceans. O Mediterraneo!

Children's Christmas Party

In the white room into which I glance,
as the afternoon fades its brown,
a tree has grown shining with silver.
A boy sucking a lollipop rides a horse.

Two girls make a cat's cradle with string.
A fat boy eats. The little girl
in the red dress with blue ribbons
in her hair opens her big eyes wide

to acclaim the admiration of mothers.
Suddenly they are all in a ring
about the tree. They throw up their white
arms waving. They sing soundless songs

to silent music for the dance.
What is all this worship? This wonder?
in which they walk and utter,
that spreads like magic

about the trees that become strange
as they are strangers to him deafened
by thin glass. Outside as soft rain falls,
as unseeing her round mouth laughs

into the night, I am for a moment
in them, it seems, but they are stars apart.

Urn Burial

(R.I.P. Scots Tongue)

It wis hardly worth peying for
a casket,
the body wis that peelie-wally,

nae bluid in't
luikit like a
scrap o' broun paper

papyrus mebbe?
nae gran eneuch
for that,

but there wis some gran mourners, the
Editor o' the *Scottish National Dictionary*,
Heid o' the Depairtment o' Scot. Lit.,
President o' the Burns Federation,
President o' the Lallans Society,
President o' the Saltaire Society,
a' present in strict alphabetical order
an
ane / twa orra Scot. Nats.

Syne cam a fuff o' win
an' liftit it oot o' the bowlie
an' hine awa,

a wee bird sang.

Dew dreep'd
on the beld heids
o' the auld men
stude gloweran
at the tuim tomb.

'She's jinkit again,
the bitch!'
said the man wi the spade.

Scots Bard

He wis taakin his breeks aff
when the thocht cam
in til's heid he
wad scrieve
a beeootiful pome

in English o' coorse.

Scots Haiku

On the completion of the Scottish National Dictionary

Noo a' thae words
are in their tomb
whan will be
the resurrectioun?

Craftsman

His being is at the pace
given by stone, wood, clay
to wrists, hands and fingers,
nor may be moved from this.

The world blazes and cries,
is shattered. He puts his hand
on clay, stone, wood,
or writes words to stay,

while the stone stars stay.

Camelias in the Snaw

A compliment for Duncan Glen

It's a fair tyave, Duncan, 'gweed kens' (my nait'ral speak)
'foo ye dee it', forever drawing blooms frae thrissles
oot o thae ingrates, wha mak black merks on a white sheet,
while ootside their wee windaes the rain pooers doon –
gien veracity tae the pathetic fallacy – aa them,
hine awa in the country o the Bens and Glens
in the clean air, or so they like tae think o Scotland,
while pitten oot the cat, an the nearby Public Incinerator
spewing intae the cessile air black flakes o snaw
tae fa gently on oor heids at Canonmills. The while
y're haudin thegither thae swalt heids, wha think
genius rins oot their pens, an his wha flee aff the hanle
at ae breath o cauld reason, wha bite the haun
that offers malt, aye double malts, forbye.
Nae doot ye dae't in hope, a blinkin hope that yet meth oot
at ony moment, but wheesht! Your lugs aye cockit
for some richt soun that still taks up a truth
lang syne incorporate in word and act, and still
in spite o cheenge, stramash and deleterious talk,
is there – an if it's there you'll print it.
An whiles, God anely kens frae where your 'whiles' are come,
you're pitten word gin word yersel, sometimes nae mair
than notin the 'braw bress-haunled coffin' or mindin
'corrieneuchin aa the evenin' but in that honest settin doun
and in the thocht, abune, ablow, aboot the thing,
the haill climactic speaks – wanhope an mair's in the yokan
o wit an' word an' deed an' lovingkindness.
There's mair than meets the blindit ee that gabs:
'nae use, nae use, it's ethnic, Scots', nae sensing
the sweet haven tae which word an thing sooms in.
When I was boy I used tae watch a skeely man
stand easy, hands in pooches, on a slopin deck,
that near the slappin water that I thocht
the boat would coup. Nae odds tae him the heavin swall,
his boatie ran on the rhythm o ocean as she slipt
doon frae the heicht o the wave intae auld Faithlie's basin.
The picter bides, cam back tae me three years sin noo
in Arizona, when oot ahint a muckle desert rock
in mornin sun, black abune the lang horizon line,
distinct in yon clear air, I saw a rider, slow an easy,

movin on till oot o sicht: syne cam evenin licht
he's back movin as gentle as the boat rocks in calm sea.
Watchin that skeely body, legs an thighs pliant
tae the saft sides o her, his hail body swack, I lookit close –
'Nae saddle!' He tellt's he'd come gey near a thoosand mile.
His reid mustang was thrawn and jibbed at bit,
would hae nae leather wechts on's flesh, but took the man.
I saw him gin that big, tuim sky and that bare land –
waur nor Scotland.

Something atween man and boards o boat and watter,
something atween man and beast and yirth
worked for, waited for, in good hairt, was richt.
And sae it is wi his in words an line.
Yet something mair's required, some extraordinar jump.
This past December in Edinburgh toun.
I saw in snaw camelias bloom.

Tree

Drives down into night
as it drives up to day.
Men are no different,
lose one, lose all.

All those dancing candles
burning their white lights
are accountable to earth,
as men grow in love from it.

Highrising for stars
knowing but concrete underfoot
he will drive a stake
through your brain.

Each day puts a foot on earth.
Each day puts a hand to a star.

Gannet

The universe is made for gannets
or the gannet for its universe –
air and sea, a bolt from the blue, a model
so modified for its purpose to kill fish
as to be maximum, machine efficient – a response
in air to the given. Given fish in water;
given gannet, high, sky high, its gimlet eye
sees fish. Six-foot wing span moves, just,
into the wind's breath, faultless, hesitates,
interrupts its plane, shuts wing and plummets
from blue into that black, a single rhythmic
movement, predestined, as the bill strikes
hard water, to kill, and will emerge
into the sun as if he was a god's angel,
feathered only for beauty of flight,
a creation of the innocent eye, purposeless
other than to be a gannet in heaven.

Why the Poet Makes Poems

*(Written to my dentist, Dr K. P. Durkacz, to explain why I failed
to keep an appointment)*

When it's all done and said
whether he is smithing away by the mad sea,
or, according to repute, silvering them in a garret
by moonlight, or in plush with a gold nib,
or plain bourgeois in a safe bungalow with a mortgage,
or in a place with a name, Paris, Warsaw, Edinburgh,
or sitting with his heart in the Highlands,
or taking time off at the office to pen a few words,
the whole business is a hangover from the men in the trees,
when thunder and sun and quake and peas in a pod
were magic, and still is according to *his* book, admitting
botany is O K for the exposition of how the buds got there,
geology for how the rocks got just like that,
zoology for the how of the animals,
biology for us kind – but that's not his game:
he's after the lion playing around with the lamb for fun.
He doesn't want to know the how, the why. It's enough
      for him to say:
'That's what's going on. The grass is jumping for joy,
and all the little fishes are laughing their heads off.'

Pursuit: Poems 1986–1998

RETURN

Departure and Departure and . . .

Someone is waving a white handkerchief
from the train as it pulls out with a white
plume from the station and rumbles its way
to somewhere that does not matter. But
it will pass the white sands and the broad sea
that I have watched under the sun and moon
in the stop of time in my childhood as I am
now there again and waiting for the white
handkerchief. I shall not see her again
but the waters rise and fall and the horizon
is firm. You who have not seen that line
hold the brimming sea to the round earth
cannot know this pain and sweetness of departure.

On the Edge – The Broch[13]

*Dedicated to the memory of Gilbert Buchan, skipper
of* The Replenish, *and to his father, James*

'To live here is to live on the edge,'
said James Buchan, 7½ Mid Street,
Inverallochy, skipper of *The Buchans*.
Gilbert's father, the name being common
but not the man, a'body kent him – 7½.[14]
Ithers micht near company his thochts,
but nae in winnan the exact words,
skipper Joseph Duthie and Love – his T name –
amang them, good men a', wha thocht
ayont their trade o' huntin herrin,
or through it, in hope a truth would oot,
beginning frae the facts o' life gien them.
James Buchan's life, handbreadths from the sea,
knew it put at nowt the vanities of class or cash.
Gilbert began from here; respect must be earned.
So he gives his boat an honest name, *Replenish*,
in hope through work on the sea's face she has

a proper return, though aye in doubt. The edge
aye there. Tae his loons it meant nae thing,
e'en when the sea brocht tae oor feet on the tide
a ba, we blootered aboot the sands or nichtfa
wioot a thocht, for a'thing was in its richt place –
the sea, the sands, the South Kirk spire, the links
wi room eneugh for 'the winds o' heiven', as the minister
pit it, tae blaw and howl hine awa ayont the bents,
owre sheenan fields o'corn tae Mormond Hill[15] that tell't
the boats whether or no their landfall was gweed.
Miles awa agin the dark hill the gryte horse[16]
shined oot fite, steen by steen a' fite,
laid doon een agin the tither: that big,
the horse, tae walk it roon, heid tae tail,
syne back, half wey yer belly's tellin,
'It's supper time:' and aye there, they say,
'frae time memorial'[17] or the like o' that.
The meen cam up and tide gaed oot
and the sands were as braid as ten
fitba pitches, and the inshore fishers
wi graips diggin the sands for sanle
for bait, and his yet at oor ba game
or they cried tae his tae help the wark.
As the sanle leapt oor hand's flasht,
but they, like lichtnin back tae their
sand hame, but again an again the graips
flung up sods o' sand and his loons catcht
the sma fish in air or they dove,
like they were siller needles richt through
thon thick sog oot o' sicht and deep doon
and never seen again. Syne we ran for hame.

Home: bed: nor-east corner: night winds beat
about the granite house. The lighthouse beam
stalks the room, is blunted on the walls,
sweeps off, and in the black dark
in sea's far-off roar, I sleep deep.
Morning – white light swims about the town.
The church spire at the top of our street
is encased in blue. The Central Public School,
encased in blue, waits for me. A white gull,
bead-eyed, sits on a lamp-post, out-stares me.
In my schoolbag is learning. It weighs one ton.

Saturday: he handed me the reins on that icy
morning at 2 Victoria Street[18] as the horse
lolloped free from Mrs McWhirter's milk delivery.
I smelt its warm leathery hide, one hand on one
big tin milk can as I stood between the two,
blowing frost like our horse, Meg, who
snorted into the air as we banged and clanged
and struck fire from the metals in the street.
Under the boards the road ran furiously
as we lifted off. Not since the chariot of the Lord
came like a whirlwind was seen such splendour
as we flew in Jim Baird's milk cart that day.
From below my grandfather's shovel beard
shouted: 'Praise the Lord!' Nothing new
in that. In these days miracles
were as common as tatties and herrin'.

The first tomorrow for me began that day,
the first time my father took me, age 7 years,
to Bruce's Look-Out. It was the first time
I saw the edge. The stair in the big, dark shed,
went up and up owre a white mountain o'saut,
syne a ladder, syne a trap door, syne oot.
Blint wi licht the cauld sun brak on my heid,
and me tellt: 'Scan the horizon.' (I had nae mind
o' meetin that word afore. Nae doot it's in the schoolbag.)
It was seven in the morning: 'What do you see?
Look to the horizon. See how it runs near round us.
Look east, now nor-nor east.' And I saw nothing
but the sea. Then I saw the endless dark line
drawn by God that separates sea from sky.
'Look again,' he said, and I saw come up
from the drowned world under the sea a mast,
a funnel, a boat. 'I see a boat!' 'Low
or high on the water?' I couldna tell, then
ithers cam. Syne I saw first one low on the watter,
then anither and anither. Come time clouds of gulls
were about each boat. All this I said to my father.
And he said: 'Right we'll go.' And sic a girnin',
an yammerin an chantin, 'forty bob, forty, forty,
fifty bob, fifty, fifty, fifty,' sic a barking
an' growlin' like dogs owre meat, deaved my lugs,
in the mart that I was deef as deef Burke

the boxer. It was heiven tae get oot an smell
the tar and ile an saut at the pierheid ootbye.
Come nicht an me in bed, and the herrin quines
yet at the guttin and me hearing the sweetest
soonds ever sangs made as thae heilan deems sang
wi words I kent nae o'. I hearkened or I was asleep.

'Ye're a grander,' glowered the fisher loon
at me and I glowered back. I never thocht
ither than the Broch loon I wis like ither loons.
'The rocket's up.' Bang, bang it gaed and his
at squeel and a'body doon the streets gan gyte
tae mak the herbour. Force 9 gale and a boat
in trouble, and afore we're there the lifeboat's awa.
But na, the lifeboat's at the herbour mou witin,
hidin' in ahint the lea o' the north breakwater,
and we kent in the open sea it would be a deathboat.
So it wited and a' the folk wited, and I cam up on
the fisher loon, and his thegither threided the crood
on the Sooth Pier, and at the heid o't
(faur eence I had catcht a conger eel)
we grippit a chine at the wa, or we'd
been blawn awa tae kingdom come. And mair
and mair folk gaithert. By the mart, hauden close,
weemen frae the Deep Sea Fisherman's Mission,
at the ready wi blankets, hot tea, dry claes,
for them near droont by the watter, and at haund
an ambulance, and fishermen by the boats tethered,
but aye creakin and groanin, for there
was nae stoppin the pouer o' that watter.
The hail toon wis there, a'body
frae granders in Strichen Road to Puddlestinkers –
a' them maistly eeseless folk, Curran Bun Chalmers
(Champion Prize Winner, Black Bun Competition, London, England),
Butcher Macfarlane, Macdonald the Grocer, and oor
school teacher, and a hantle ithers – but a' witin,
quaet, and naething tae see but watter –
heich hills o't thrashin ootside the herbour mou,
lumps o' watter loupin the breakwater and ower
the tap o' the herbour beacon that ends the steen wa.
And his! – we're starin oor een oot stracht
afore's – sometimes nae sky, jist black watter.
Stare we micht hopin for sicht o' somethin

that meth be boat, but naething. Then sudden
she's there. Sudden she's gone aneath a wall o' watter,
and again she's there, that near I saw the *FR*
on her, then gone. This time nae come back,
finished, I thocht, but na, she's heich
on tap o'a wave that maun carry her stracht on,
aye and be smashed tae bits on the beacon wa.
The skipper steers her clear o't and noo
she's richt in mid-channel. We haud oor braeth –
a'body, and the lifeboat settles a meenit atween
beacon and pier, but nae eese, the cross-wave
cacht the *Golden Harvest* – say I thocht her name –
and swept awa oor hope. Still we wited, still
stared across the watters gettin dark.
And she was there further oot, syne doon, syne
up again, syne ae moment at the herbour mou,
her bow pints stracht at his, at the Sooth Pier heid!
The skipper kent a' thing, kent the shore wave's
back-wash and, bidin his time, kent it, and drove
the boatie through: and a' the folk cheerin
and greetin and dancin, and haudin een till
anither wioot a thocht, wioot a care if he
was Puddlestinker or e'en cam fae Peterheid.

'Not in the storm but in a calm night
and the stars shining down; the vast expanse
of waters, throws his thought back on fishermen.
He is in another world separated and isolated.
To live here is to live on the edge.'[19]

House with Back-Garden

Our granite house
by the sea – never
out of its roaring or
shushing or hacking cough –
stood steady as any rock.

A good house with good people
in it; who looked after it,
and us. Everything there
was in its right place,
except us boys, of course,
though we knew where
we ought to be.

The way to the back green
was through the big trellised
gate. It wobbled open
when pushed or kicked,
which we did. We would

rush into the back garden
to kick a ball on my Dad's
lawn, a whole football team
of us. We kicked it to pieces.
Father watched us kick his
green grass to pieces,
which he had watered
and cut, and got just right.

He did not stop our game,
just watched from the window.
I went into the house. He said:
'My poor lawn.' I cried. He said:
'Never mind you enjoyed yourselves.'
And then laughed. No grudge.
He patted me on the head.

The Face

In the dark narrow hallway of Father and Mother
on the mahogany table, a silver salver;
on it, etched, a woman with hair streaming
in the wind, where was no wind. The date is 1917.
My cousin Alister has returned from the trenches.

His glengarry is on the silver salver.
I see his khaki puttees tight about his legs.
He speaks in a deep voice. No-one else speaks.
No-one else has the right to speak
While the soldier from the trenches speaks.

Are there legs inside the khaki bandages?
His eyes shine a little with grey lights.
He has a moustache. His gun had a bayonet.
I have a dagger like a bayonet.

I press the bayonet against my chest.
The blade disappears but there is no blood.
Perhaps the soldier's bayonet is like that.
This war is a silent picture that is still.

It is all in the *London Illustrated News*.
Page by page the soldiers stand to attention
for ever. The generals are on horseback.
They never move. In the silver salver
I see the face of a child, it weeps.

Father and the Silver Salver

As was his custom at
approx. 9a.m. he returned
from the yard for coffee,

would plant his cap on the
silver salver on the hall table
and announce he was home.

He'd been on the go from
6a.m. to yard, office, harbour.
He brought into the house

salt airs, left on the door-mat
sequins of herring scales
that flashed in sunlight.

On this fine morning the cap
did not leave the hand.
No salver. He minded

he'd met a couple, man
pushing a two-wheeled,
flat-topped float, wife

walking alongside with shut face.
On top a pile of rags, clothing,
mebbe all their worldly goods.

Down Victoria Street he went.
No sighting. The way south,
Saltoun Place, out of town,

he overtook them, paced them,
the while one hand lifting
the rags, slipping from them

the silver salver. No word spoken.
They went their way, he his.

Cliff Face Erosion

'e cosi esisti' – Montale
for my brother, Robert – il miglior linguista

Fae that blin mappa mundi face;
scartit, I wud look awa bit that
tae its lang daith ma face
is bondit, an will-na win awa.

I am old. Yet the breathing intimacies
of air, those inspirations from the forever
fresh wildernesses of sea; even the sea pink
I picked from the marram grass as child,
has carried through the years unfearful,
trusting, secured through time into this now,
this moment of putting pen to paper as if
this wholeness, indestructible, outdated
time and gave to us a permanence of being.

You tell me what I would not know.
From the frail page you stare at me
with the authority of millions of years,
and I am diminished to a point not
to be picked out even by that
electronic scan that determines existences
light years from this planet; and you
present indifferently substance and
ephemera, darknesses and lights, yet
no more are you the bastion that you were,
resisting and denying access to sea's force,
the great wave falling from you, and you
remained yourself. Now to the gnawing salt,
the flux of waters, cross-fire of elements,
you concede. Ravaged, penetrated, scuffed,
deep-graven – your face is witness,
as is the human face, to the years.
I look upon your face and it is mine.
I look upon you and marvel.

Night-Fall

Nae soun: nae sea soun,
Fit wye nae sea soun?
Hid the deid-chack knockit
i the nicht an a' the toun
slipt intae the lang sleep?
Me, a bairn, wakt, an nae peep
o licht fur nae sea soun sang.

Most times the shore and the sea
is telling us little enough, food
for one, another in the summer,
even in our cold North, a place
for mothers in creaking deck chairs,
children clattering their tin pails
waiting for sand-pies or little fish.
But once as night fell he was there,
the tide 'that far oot – an nae soun –
cud it iver come back? an black rocks
niver seen afore, an I maun be there.
I slipt ma haun intae the cald watter
aneath the black wrack, an feel ma wye
intae the crack on the rock, an there
wis a gryte partan. Ma fingers traivelt
on an on on the shall. It wint on foriver.
Niver wis sic a crab. Feart I ran
for hame. The braith gaed oot o me.
I stopt, an took a keek back.'

Dark fell on sands and rock,
but the waters were bright holding
light to themselves. The sea
had ceased its terrible proclamations.
It was as if it had yielded its powers
to another order, one hardly guessed at,
nor to be seen from our disturbed universe,
yet now some thought that they had glimpsed
that long-sought peace that lay beyond our hopes.

The Herbour Wa, MacDuff

For George Gunn

The wa! – the face o blunt rebuttal –
sea's girn, yelloch, yammer, snash, greet
an then thunner that wud smore a' – this
the wa took on, whiles the squat beacon licht
signalled hope fae its steen stack tae boats
storm-driven, that, but for it, meth stravaig
heid-on tae wa, an that's an en o't,
an them aboard. Exac timin, steady hauns, keen ee,
tae haud her deid-mid the run o watter tween piers.
The Provider, wi a wecht o haddock, cod, ling, sole,
twa monkfish an a conger we cud duin wioot,
netted saxty mile nor-nor-east Kinnaird,
the nor wun at her stern, heids in atween the gap,
nae a thocht, nae a doot at the rin-in, driven
bi thon hard race. They're for hame, diesel pooer,
as the boats, steam an sail, through a' the years.

Haiku for John Ferguson

Rector of Fraserburgh Academy

Coming home
to the sea-town
shared interests
much understanding

The sun leans
on the low landscape
the sea is kindly
affection stirs

The flat stone
in Kirkton Kirkyard
by the sea's mouth
spells our endless end

Mist

Mist shrouds the Firth
contains all, allows entry
only to the finger
of the mind, contains
time past, hard-backs
resistant to wear of water,
predators predating all
kind, or simples, uni-cellular
expression, or us mulched to
such fineness as that transparent
air in stratosphere provides.

Moss Agate

As if the North green-weedy sea
had entered in and met the South,
unctuous and vinous, suffusing reds
with subtle lights of plum.

And this is stone and common.
No moonstone omen from eternity
but sea-washed, bound for Scotland
when the cosmic pot was on the boil.

Something between the soft, wild lights
of a winter sky and any careless
autumn afterthought, now transfixed,
like Leonardo's famous smile.

Ian in the Broch [20]

To Ian McNab, civil engineer and singer, who sang the Iona Gloria
in St Giles' Cathedral, Edinburgh, at a commemoration of the
1400th anniversary of the death of Saint Columba, memorably.

Returned, but never away.
Rain storms at arrival, but
sun prevails. Brightness is all,
white on the wings of the glancing
fulmar. Wave breaks, white light
shakes from its blue. All one
to him at the centre, an internet
in himself: hardly a step
at the harbour, and another
McNab has a word with him.
This is the flower of friendships
engendered in the generations,
caught up now in this talk-talking
town, aye, toun, 'fou's aa?'
'fit's deein?', and on again
as if heaven were not about him
in this place in time, where
the running boy runs forever
in the mind, yet he would know,
know his place, know how
the lighthouse light projects its beam,
timely, exact on the dark waters.
But look at the tapered rollers
bearing the great weight of the
gyrating mirrors, steel supports,
that issue the light to all seamen.
Now he walks the town simply
as if the common talk's enough,
but from him, from head and lips –
GLORIA!

FOLK

Responsibilities

For Stephen Strachan

The little boy with the little drum
gave it the exact tap.
'I tap it and tap it,'
said the boy unsmiling
for the responsibility was great.

If the rat-tat-tat had not been
exact
on time
all
was lost.

He stood alone
before
the eight players of
Pencaitland Primary School Jazz Band.

The face of the boy listened
to the silences between
the beats.
When
all ended and the applause
broke the bonds of the band
he heard nothing of it.

His eyes stared in wonder
as his heart beat out
the exact
tap tap.

Invocation

o a thae gaitherins i the High Street
an Canongate betokinin the Scottish Poetry Library
for Tessa[21]

Wha cud hae thocht that I
trimmlin on the lip o time,
ma licht at peep, cud yet
staun here an harken
the multitude murmurs risin
an fain at derk frae closes,
vennels, howfs, dens o sin,
the like that poet chiels hae haunted
owre a' the years – an noo a' gaithered
here ablow. Aince Scott, the boy, his mou
ticht shut, in Sibbald's libr'ry, gawpt
at yon chiel, Burns, nor daurd
say words. This was a true respec:
while doun the Canongate the bard
himsel peyed oot his hard won
puns in stane to honour Fergusson,
an yet a third jined in, Stevenson.
Een a fourth in oor time
stude at the grave, Garioch.
The auld toun gied them drink
an words, an sangs, an hellish deeds.
Sae as we stap oot this nicht
think nocht o the flim-flam-fleerie
lichts, that ken nocht o this
maist wanchancy past, that's
in us noo: as we bide here
at *The Warld's En* maun harken
til anither soun an lat thae
whisperin delicates, the lang thochts,
the breathin o the spirit o
Tessa's rare 'Medusa' sang.
Tak tent, harken, an let
the new quaet voice be here.

Epistle 1: To Edwin Morgan

A response to Edwin Morgan's invitation to submit a poem for publication in New Writing, Scotland, *which he and Carl MacDougall edited.*

Your letter, the best thing
that happened for a time, since I
am at odds with my self, and it
brought me momentarily together.
BUT doubt steps in between
the pen and paper as to whether
any good cd come from a body
too young for my age.
                                    It's a
pleasure to be with you now as I am,
to see your smile in my mind
as I do now, and to pride my
self that I might have some thing
still to bring out my oddity.

No more journeys; and when I
am thinking back to the last
N.C., U.S.A. affray I cannot
stay my eye on the blue butterfly,
handsbreadth winged on the red
azaleas by the campus lakeside:
it takes off for habitation
for blacks, which I, misguided
surprised, find at a dead end
where the road turns to dirt track
running by the railline (freight
only). I shd have been on tother side
happy with whites in their forever cars.
STILL I had a southern breakfast
(7.30 – 10.30a.m.) with Mary de Rachewiltz,[22]
E.P.'s daughter on a quiet spring day
in a colonial, one-storey, white-pillared
home (as the Americans would say). Sat
in the portico, with terra cotta colour
steps, flanked by two Romanesque urns,
white. Cool. She wore a pale green dress.
Beyond the garden, azaleas and shrubs in it,
nothing, rough grass, weeds. A tornado had
taken away the firestation outbye

and all the other buildings, so
there we were in a nothing.
'What thou lovest well remains
        the rest is dross'
the motto for her *Discretions*.
Was she mistaken to pour out
her love on Babbo? Still does as she
annotates *The Cantos*. I say Joseph Macleod.
'Joseph Gordon Macleod wrote *The Ecliptic*,'
she quotes the line from the *Cantos*,
'And I know nothing of him.' I oblige,
remark we were to visit Pound. Venice.
All arranged. Pound ill. 'He came back
to Brunnenburg.' No more spoken till.
'Come to Brunnenburg.' I tremble
at the thought of that high Schloss
with suffering Pound and his women;
have enough ado keeping my own
ghosts under the floor. This house
creaks with them. Yours, affec. G.B.

Epistle 2: *Response to an Invitation to Meet a Memory*

On 24 September 1989, from 2–4pm,
in Alderston Auditorium, Kansas Union,
we will remember Professor Edward L. Ruhe,
who died on 29 June 1989. Please join us
for this memorial service and for
the reception to follow.
                    Department of English, University of Kansas,
                        to George Bruce, Edinburgh, Scotland

May 1982, met him, and then only thrice or so,
nor ever after. He was at the table next to us,
Fellows' Dining hall, National University, Canberra.
Alone, uneasily he smiled; unprompted introduced himself
as: 'Ruhe – commonest name in German cemetries – Peace.'
The humour was not lost when unpeaceably he drove
round roundabouts along straightways on the wrong
side of the road. We survived lorries, cars, long-vehicles,
while he talked, talked of 'the burial customs of Aboriginals',

switching on a bend of the road to 'Smart – Christopher
Smart of *Song to David* fame, but *"Jubilate Agno!"'*
As he turns his head he gives out the line:
'For the mouse is a creature of great personal valour.'
The voice holds on course. He is the professor in essence,
enquirer and admirer of the inhabitants of the planet,
forever strange to him, yet kin.

                        Afterwards I looked at
the kangaroo, the guana, galah, pelican, lyre-bird,
and saw how peculiar were the brown sparrows
fluttering in the dust at my Scottish door-step.

Epistle 3: To Maurice and Joyce Lindsay

To hansel their new home on Milton Hill

The ghosts of your homes wander through
my address books. The aches of iron trams,
juddering and squealing through Hillhead,
founder on your step at Athole Gardens.
Elegant Southpark Avenue fades into night.
At Gartocharn dogs howl, children tumble,
horses nose your doors, the loch stays
at a distance; the broad parks of Annan –
gone. I remember a red gown, a girl
in misty St Andrews, who had, she said,
'a friend called Maurice Lindsay'.
Before the unchanging features of friendship
the irritations of the silly world
vanish. Now stand solitary on the hill
as the tides run silently below;
each moment holds our being – this know.

Epistle 4: To Ruby (5), Holly (3), Shirley and Timothy Cumming.

Written on a Christmas card reproducing
Hunters in the Snow by Bruegel the Elder

Just as it was when Icarus fell
out of the sky, as Peter Bruegel saw it,
the great adventure ending miserably,
no-one paid any attention – the ploughman
went on ploughing, the shepherd shepherding,
the fisherman fishing, the ship puffing
its sails for somewhere else, so it is
with *Hunters in the Snow.* They pass
the women warming at the fire, who give no heed;
a cart with provender heads for the village;
a woman, back bent with a load of faggots
is crossing a bridge, snow crowned, earth
bound in whiteness, sky beams back
the winter message. Her heart is on
the dry stick blaze in the hearth of home.
It is the play upon the ice for old
and young that holds each to their moment,
as the bird of prey holds to the sky
forever there in the miraculous landscape.
No-one looks up, all are busy being
themselves. Good people, all!
Be yourselves, and time will stop
for you in the dance of Holly and Ruby.

15 December 1996

Epistle 5: A Thank-You to John Bellany

For his card (Christmas 1997), especially for the painting
of three fishermen standing on the deck of their boat[23]

Their trade's to trawl the seas,
hunt fish, gut fish, land fish –
no sweet job, so some will
to God in heaven, some to booze
to keep them 'richt for the morn'
to face wind and water and doubt.
So they contain the rough deal
of life they've got, make it
look easy – 'that's the wey it is,'
but, John, you plant the three
fronting us from the deck, and one
half-hidden in the hold's dark,
who've tholed the cauld of day
and night since Noah's flood.
The big bag-net spewed out
the mixter-maxter o a' kinds,
spattered the boards with blood;
oilskins, gum-boots, hands, fingers
flecked with blood. No silver darlings
now, no red-spotted plaice now, no
fluke soft-gliding on the sand, no
flashing ling, no staring cod, no
glittering shoals o a' thae peerie fish
that soom in perfect harmony thegither.
Job done. Each, straight upright, strains
to be man, carrying the weight
of the wealth of the prodigality
of sea. They prepare a table,
offering it to us for squander.
One, mouth agape, a silent agony,
another, arms rigid, fingers clutch,
but at the centre of the trinity,
the Christ-man with the three-pointed fish,
the skate. He clamps it to his body.
They are in judgement, but judge.
The betrayal is ours.

Soup and Sherry

It was 3.30 in the afternoon, mid-November,
and I was calling on Bill Gillies
(Sir William Gillies, R.S.A., R.A. etcetera):
'Come in,' he says, 'We'll have soup.
You won't be drinking and driving
so we'll have sherry.' Didn't like
the idea of the combination, but
the lentil soup was hottering
on the stove so there was nothing for it
but swallow it with the sherry.
There was a painting on the easel
of Temple, the village where we were.
It didn't look like the rainy street
off which I'd just come. In it
the moon was up and silvering
the length of it, pavement, tarmac road,
squat houses, and touching up
two black trees, winter trees,
but each twig starting from its branch
as if Spring were in it. I looked out
the window. Nothing like the painting.
No glimmering windows along the street.
He was stirring the soup. He didn't look up.
'I catched a painting last night.'
I could see him casting on the Esks,
North Esk, South Esk, Leithen Water, Falla.
How many paintings got away? 'Soup's ready.'
How many poems slip back into my dark sea?

Gillies

Self-portrait. 1941. Oil on canvas. 86 by 70cm.
Scottish National Gallery of Modern Art

Did he know as he put the self on canvas
that stood there merely holding the brushes,
looking from there back at the stranger,
the light was upon him and about him;
about him light touched by enlightenment,
the painting claiming the silence,
creating that to which the final word aspires?

Mindin David Murison

'It's nae mows,' he said tae me
fin' I hid tell't him that a bodie
wis jist 'kenspeckle' an he hid said,
'Na, ill teenit' o the man fa made
a monkey o wir tongue. Aye, bit said
wi twinklin ee. Sae I mind
this humorous chiel, thrawn till's daith,
niver gien tae bleat aboot his sel,
bit coorse on aa that stuid atween him
an the grite en o chievin the last wurd
i the buik o Scots. Syne he wud be
king o aa, his heid repository
o territory that raxed fae Picts tae present,
fae John o Groats tae Tweed.
Sic a wecht o warlds tae cairry,
an that he did maist lichtly.
That deen hame, tween roarin seas
an Mormond Hill. Bit niver feenished.
He tripped alang, sma-boukit man,
gryte hertit, mair than ony meth unnerstan.

At Mayakovsky's Statue[24]

Ae shoulder heisted
tae ca doun
the deid warld o offices –
Konfer, Konfer, Konfer!

It's nae as easy as that.

So he sticks oot a chin –
he'll tak the warld on't:
bit that glower kens
it's nae that easy
to be
'a clood in breeks'.

He wud mairch
oot o's orra duds
straight intae history.

By God, he did:
noo stauns a stane man
at this Moscow corner,
Mayakovsky Square.

Peace

Pairty at a Collective Tea Fairm, Georgia, 1973

The Russian Orthodox Christian Georgian Communist,
Member o the Supreme Soviet,
cheerman o the pairty
heistit his glass
tae me.

Uttered.

Forty Baptist Kirk Georgian Communist basses
heistit their glasses.

      Uttered.

      I ken nae Georgian.

      At the stert o the feast
      twenty-twa bottles stude on the table.
      At the hinner-end o't
      thirty-twa stude.

      Then I kent a'.
      Noo I ken nae Georgian.

The Crescent

In memory of Martin Prestige (1935–79) at 4 Warriston Crescent

[Martin Calder Prestige: 'His death, at the early age of 44, removes from the world of developmental neurobiology one of its most incisive minds and able investigators.' *Nature* 29 Nov. 1979]

This is a place called home –
home because we live here
looking at the park where girls
crack their hockey-sticks together
and boys play football furiously

because the Water of Leith at
our back door at a moment's notice
blows itself up and runs off in fine
fettle with ducks, pianos and any old
iron, then deflates to the burn it is

because conversation interrupts
shopping expeditions we know
people this way. Suddenly one
is no longer there and we are not
what we were. This one now

whose slight form moving with
difficulty looked in for a few years,
slipped into several minds and hearts.
We, as usual, thought nothing of this
till suddenly his attentive ear,

his glance, interested, through the shining
windows of his glasses, was no longer
present. There was an impression of
serenity – it stretched from him
all the way to 33.[25] People smiled

and didn't know why. He honoured us
with his suffering, never shown.
Now there remains the slight space of
his awkward walk which cannot quite
be filled.

Elizabeth in the Garden

'It is,' she said, 'a windflower,[26] Japanese.'
The white windflower at the wall is still.
We sit in the moment as if we'd
stepped outside the running world
and made a here-and-now that stopped
the ripened apple's drop to earth,
caught in that round moment that sought
a word, yet dared not say for
on my mortal breath the word would
perish. Would God that this, this word,
the Word would spread its timeless time,
but that Rwanda's cries and all its kind
here and about, proclaim the self-destructive mind.

Words for Jenni, 8 July 1996

*8 July 1996. A pendant for my granddaughter visiting
Thailand while I was at Lake Maggiore*

That day the lake was silver, hardly
an airy whisper about and you
were in the company of Buddha.
Perhaps his serenity discovered you.
So it was here as the chemistry of heaven
suffused the waters with a thousand colours.
This day may the beatitude be yours.

Castle Tioram, Loch Moidart

The tide comes in and empties the castle
of all but its bloody memories. The tourists
are gone, the last bustling to the shore
before the tide cut-off, leaving their litter.
Paper bags spin up draughty holes and out,
whisked out to sea. Lords of the Isles
lived here, thinking to themselves – forever.
Gone. What human kind were they anyway?
Pride, courage, cruelty in them, no doubt.
Evening – the loch stills. In its shimmer
Tioram trembles. From the dark cube laughter,
echoes of children, the new invaders –
Andrew, Ken, Karen, Jennifer, Ben –
a play pen for them. Night,
skraichs – the sea birds have it for themselves.

At Lake Maggiore

5am, 28 June 1996, Hotel du Parc, Stresa

Oggi aurora con dita rosa.
Dove, dove gli strumenti alati
di celebrazione felicita?

This day 'the rosy-fingered dawn'.
Where, where are the winged
instruments of celebration?

In the Train

'Are you going to Glasgow?' he said,
as only a man from Glasgow could say.
There was nowhere else for this train to go
so I said nothing. Neither 'yes' or 'no',
but stared at the grey man in grey, grey hair,
grey face, his chin and his nose so close,
as if no teeth between, his eyes shut tight,
his lips drawn tight to let nothing get in.
Then as the train sped on its way the light

broke new, spreading its beams on fields
of stubble and green on this November day,
but all I saw was a faceless man,
thin flesh a cover for bones. Till Glasgow came.
He opened grey eyes, and bright they shone. 'Glasgow!'
he bawled with a laugh that shoved off wrong,
and Sauchiehall Street was one long song.

'I come from Shetland'.
Time melts as if before acetylene's force.
Eyes open on micaceous beach.
Tides at a race strand
a whale. Skies high with light,
with birds harsh in chorus strew
the air – talk, talking of gulls,
terns, guillemots, puffins and petrels.
Beneath – the provident seas that
would sustain multitude, but that
we came.

Vibrations

'Be nocht hoity-toity'

You'll mind on the gran tenor
wha's tap note brak the gless
on the table-tap intae twa thoosand pieces.
You'll mind on 'the classic case'
o the wa's o Jericho.
And then there wis the hen
that look't Mrs McPhee
straucht in the ee,
an she split.

Noo abody has their vibrations,
witin in the back-shop
or unner the bed
or spewed oot sudden
frae a shiny computer.

So, watch yer step this fine mornin,
my mannie.

PURSUIT

Weys o Self-Preservin Natur

We socht for bait on the bay sands, braid
ahint the far-oot sea, whiles at nicht-fa
and the mune up. As the sanle leapt
oor haunds flasht, and they like lichtnin
back to their sand hame, but agen and agen
the graips threw up sods o sand
and his loons cacht the sma fish in the air
or they dove, like they were siller needles,
richt through thon thick sog oot o sicht
and deep doon and never seen agen,
and we thocht naething o't.

We socht for safticks for bait, green backs
noo slippit oot their hard shalls that floatit
in the shallow pools whaur the flukes bided
on the sand, *that* like the sand that nae ee
kent ane frae tither, til lang staunin cauld
in the watter a ripple kittled the sole
o my fit and I cacht her and pit her in my pail
and saw the speckles on her like sand
and teemed her back and saw her soom awa,
and we thocht naething o't.

Yestreen oor telly took's tae keek aneath
the watters o Chesapeake Bay to goggle at
a monster screen-size crab witin on's love
but she scrawled by him on the sand
and oot the frame, syne in agen and oot
the tither side, and in agen as she were
blin tae him and what he's aifter. Sudden
his preen-heid een on stalks stare oot.
Sudden he hauds her tae him in's iron airms:
syne naething: nae muve. For twa lang days
she's in the jile: syne her carapace, jist that,
heists itsel aff her body, sae it seems, floats free
yet agen they're rock-still till she, gentle
– and delicate in her saft skin – turns ower
aneath her man; and he nae monster noo,

his grip lat go, wites, respectfu o his dame,
or frae her sel soom up thae eggs
that mak himsel tae spew oot the milk
tae fertilise, ensure the continuity
o the tribe *Brachyura*: this the climax
o their ploy, they unkennin that I and millions
geck, and whiles I watch, my guid-wife puts
into this auld haund a clam-shall fossil
brocht tae Edinburgh frae Chesapeake Bay,
one hunder and fifty million years auld.
Aince there stirred under this shall – life.
I thocht o the bearers o the chyne o life
that would gang on and on or lang deid this haund,
and yet the mair I vrocht at thocht
the mair I kent hoo peerie was the thocht.

Blin boozed-up his faither struck him
time and time agen, and he was oot the door.
He struck oot sooth. The lift gaed the wrang wey,
turned aff tae a side-road, syne intae a sma glen.
He slept in the lea o a stane dyke, a burn ran by.
Mornin. The mist was risen afore him, mixed in
wi the floorish o gean and blackthorn: bird sang,
teuchats flapped aboot the derk plooed fields,
lambs bleat frae the green field tither side.
He gaed nae heed: he's on his way tae the A68.
She tell't him the A68's for lifts. Noo
in Lon'on toun she's in the moneys there,
and her wi freens. 'Mither o God!' she said,
tae her pimp, 'I'll no dae that.' And him,
'Christ then ye're for't. I'v dune wi you.'
Hoo mony gang their weys tae the gowden city?
He fund his wey til't a'richt. A wrang!
Whaur, whaur his hame, his shall o comfort,
his ingan residence o love? There by the staney banks,
Sweet Thames run softly til I end my song,[27]
he bides aneath the airches o Westminster Brig.
Up-by the Palace o Westminster, Mither o Parliaments,
and mither at the tap eidently protectin her brood
frae the storms o divisions in retour for lealty,
as we ken noo, seein their doups jig up and doon
frae green upholstery, theirsels upholstered weel eneuch,
makin just laws preservin them that his and them

that hisna as they are, but mair-so the noo.
This their naitral hame, if no quite that, the place
where maist they ken themsels, at the hert o Lon'on toun.
London, *Sovereign of cities, semeliest in sight.*
Above all ryvers thy Ryver hath renowne,
Whose beryall stremys, pleasaunt and preclare,
Where many a swanne doth swymme with wyngis fare.
Upon thy lusty Brigge of pylers white
Been merchauntis full royall to behold.[28]
And upon heich the pillars o Society: plc,
wha haud the cairts, them a', and unnerneath discairds,
members o the Free Air Sociability Society,
unlimited – free stinks, free quarters, ludgins
shared by a' creepin things – winos, wide-boys,
crack addicts, chancers wha didna tak their chance,
traivellers wha's traivellin's ended, a deein man
wi a dog, a lassie wi a bairnie at her breist –
and him, nae prodigal, but pit-oot: his nicht-hoose,
dwallin place, a shauchle o caird-board boxes.
A stound o pitie gaed tae the hert, quo Lorimer.[29]
For him was nae retour, nae forgien faither,
nae hame in the black hole o angst whaur
bided his progenitors; they wha catapulted him
intae this life or daith or mixter-maxter o the baith.
'Faither, forgie them, for they kenna what they dae'
The crab, the clam, the sanle, fluke unkennan ken.

The Chair[30]

Poet's and Painter's

chair – a seat for one person
Oxford English Dictionary
cheer, chear, cheir – chair
Concise Scots Dictionary
kathedra – a seat
Greek–English Lexicon

Greek gives the chair dignity, suggests cathedral,
a bishop's seat, hieratic, 'dim religious light', but
'Poets's Chair?' No! Na! in Scots 'Makar's Cheer',
frae whilk the makar Robert Henryson began the anely
great, tragic makar's tale in Lallan tongue.
The Testament of Cresseid, screivin in winter.

> 'I mend the fire and beikit me about
> Then tuik ane drink my spreitis to comfort
> And armit me weill fra the cauld thair out.'

Sic a cheer for guid Maister Henryson, teacher,
mann sober be as fits the man, durable, siccar
as the aik frae whilk it cam, its seat comfortable
whaur a man meth set his doup lang hours,
legs nae funcy, at joints tenon to mortise firm,
airms fluent in style, supportive, convenient
for the poet while deep in thocht, or drappin aff,
or in a dwaum seekin solace frae warldly cares,
afore the neist blast o words, thunderin his lugs,
comes roarin tae his pen. Sic a cheer had I
and thocht the seasoned wuid would last for aye.
Syne agin a' natur it cam to be anither *thing*.

Wife It couldna be but him that knocked the cheer
tae kingdom come. Nae meenit still
but raxed himsel, one wey an tither,
forard an back, his pen in's nieve,
warslin wi yon cheer, tormentin't, daein
a fandango on the flair, stumpin aroon
the room huntin ae word, a ithers bein wrang,
syne pechin at the desk, heid bowed doon,
he thinks he's cacht it in his haund,
he's balanced on twa legs, the hinder twa in air,
the puir thing strivin tae haud thegither,
taigelt wi his sinews, wrigglin tae get awa.
Sudden he pu's the cheer aneath his bum,
he thinks he's got the measure, the richt beat
o the words: now they'll sing for him, groan,
moan, smile, lauch for him: he's happy,
awa wi't – ower the mune, gone tae
a dear green place (he says) whaur peace
breathes ower a, leavin ahint in sair travail
the cheer that's taen frae him his fevered fears.

Poet Na, na. I sat me doon on't fine and cosy
cocked an ee at my braw time-piece –
snoozing time for me in my auld cheer
that cam tae me from my good business father,
a man o sense, who had nae time
for flim-flam poesie but 'held straight on
for deals'. He was 'well thought of', respected,
wearin a black top-hat at funerals. Syne
in mid-thocht I'm gruppit frae ahint,
roon my middle and ablow – a randy customer
wha, octopus-like, flings its airms,
there's mair than twa, aboot my breist,
twines its legs roond mine – I'm in
a straight jacket – bangs my heid
shoves it tae this white paper on the desk,
and in my lugs words o the cheer commence:
'Sgriobh! Scrieve! Write!' – the command
in a' three leeds, the ancient tongue, Gaelic,
language of the Garden of Eden (the Gaels say)
the Lallan tongue, my ain, aince the King's Scots.
English as spoken here in Scotland: but scrieve what?
Whispers, whispers, 'la chaise du peinture,'
The Yellow Chair, Vincent's chair.

In Arles that Spring the lark rose
from the cornfield to sing for him.
Skies rejoiced, sang their blue for him.
The petals of the orchard showered about him,
each blossoming on the knife, the brush,
in the chemistry of paint. In Arles
from dawn to dusk the sun shone for him.
He painted the yellow sun. He painted
the sower as the sun drove earthwards
and the hand of the sower was the hand
of the god of creation. He painted
the sway in the corn as the organic
earth-force ordered him. The vault
made its statement, no words for such utterance.
The charge set, the fuse lit, earth leapt,
the onrush in a gyre spiralled the cypresses.
Skies hurried their thunders in oes and whorls,
hurtled him. In his wonderment he became
them. No respite. The eyes of the stars were his,
entered him, force unleashed, leashed,
channelled to brain, hand, encounter
with canvas – all to be rejoiced in. No:
such unfair advantage – a universe expounding
its force, had done so in quake, volcano,
earth-crust opening, basalt flow, rock,
through geological time, now a concentrate
in him, demanding him to contain such violences,
trap all in the small rectangle. There was
blood at his listening ear, blood at his eyes.
His astounded look was in the black cloud of crows
darkening its yellow: but about and about the town
bright undulating meadows, a yellow sea – buttercups,
'I shall paint my little house yellow. I want it
to be the house of light for everyone.
Let the sun walk into my house.'
The sunflowers spoke to him:
'L'oeil du soleil, c'est l'oeil de Dieu.'
I shall put them on the walls of my room.
He put twenty burning suns in the atelier
for glory: their hosannas possessed him,
but in the bedroom 'square deal furniture,
the wooden beds are like fresh butter.'
Two chairs had their beginnings in a tree

nearby and in the grasses of the field,
products of the slow labour of country people.
He stared at the chair where Gauguin had sat,
looked long at it where Gauguin had left
his pipe and ash on it. He'd painted the chair;
now he painted a picture of it:
'a wooden straw-covered chair yellow
all over standing on red tiles against a wall'.
Planted now by the painter's hand,
firm, sturdy, settled, no grace
but authority, seen with the eye
of imagination and love, it proposes
no time past, no future, but is.

Pursuit[31]

Dedicated to Elizabeth Cumming who made possible the poem by
her gift, 'Letters on Cézanne' by Rainer Maria Rilke

The incarnation of the world *as a thing carrying conviction*, the portrayal of a reality
become imperishable through his experiencing of the object – this appeared the purpose of
his inmost labours . . . and was once more on his road . . . beyond the studio to a valley . . .
in front of which soared the mountain range of Saint Victoire.

Rilke on Cézanne, in a letter to Clara Rilke,
Paris, 9 October 1907

Surely all art is the result of one's having been in danger, of having gone through an
experience all the way to the end where no one can go any further.

Letter from Rilke to Clara Rilke,
Paris, 24 June 1907

Search, he must, in words, by words,
through words, yet never the Word.
None possessed that, could not, for
the act of possessing was itself
stained, yet one move towards
that point of certainty might be
made, but not through the versimilitude
of changing, growing, dying nature.
As Virgil, as guide, to Dante,
so Cézanne to Rilke. Versimilitude
gives, yields nothing, but seek

with the mental eye that admits
from each thing, creature of
earth or sky or water, its own
effulgence, at whose source is
the single cell. Was the germinating
nucleus the icon of today? Look
on the mass of mountain, style,
shape, line, colour, yet look
inward to the core of being, self,
but look selflessly. See Spring come
again and again in the green shoots:
see the flush of Summer in the rose:
see the flame of the Fall from tree
casting its lavish hues, yet still see
nothing in unstilled time, but to still
the rushing tumble of nature in word
or stroke of brush – could he
who held the painter's knife or brush,
carry, transform that meaning
into the sentence or square
of canvas? Will the curtain of the mind
withdraw and transparency be his?
Look again in the iron bond of Winter,
look to the bare bones of tree, of bush,
blasted, of barbed rose stems. Wait.
And the 'house of being'[32] provides.
'Concealed gardeners' inhabit the trees,
he said. Blake named them 'Angels'
as the silence of growth spoke to him.
Morning, noon and late, an old man
left the decent town of Aix.
Montagne Sainte Victoire, a presence
at a distance, did not disturb it,
but demanded him, Paul Cézanne,
to make the same sojourn through
ignorant streets. Insensate,
the populace howled at him. He,
who did not belong. This their daily
benediction at his setting out.
Children danced about him, sang,
hurled stones at him. He was
bound for the country where was
'l'atelier à Les Lauves'. Apples

strewed the floor, and would stay there.
They weighed as much in the mind
in paint as the hill. All belonged
to the one great whole, but on.
Cluttered, the way awkward, narrowing:
bush, tree, vegetable growth, ages old,
wide-spread, yield variants of green,
but mention of habitation, pink
roof-tops claim touches of attention
and beyond, the mountain's ever-changing
blue – but stones held the eye, the mind,
their differentiating thrust, counter
and spare, sometimes rust, sometimes
honey, reddening in the morning sun,
all known to him from life's beginning.
As boy he knew the challenge, the bruise
of bare boulder, limestone rock, grit
of sandstone, cuts in terrain, precipice
drops. He'd gone beyond Château Noir,
clambered up les Roches Barrées, then
as Sainte Victoire possessed his sight,
his first notation, first confrontation
on a sheet of white paper
that told what had not been done.
Now mind reached from the frail body
to contain all – the vertical pointing
stones, the horizontal wall of boulders.
To-fro the eye went, held, momentarily
within their bulk and firm outline.
All noted. To each and all, he,
the image-creator, maker, responds.
From any given form from earth, sky or water,
he could not turn away. Accept, he must.
To reject any is to reject all,
would imperil that state of grace
that granted him his innocent stroke.
Out of outcrops grew the Mountain.
A great line swept across the canvas
to the airy top. On this day sun shone,
revealed the muscled balks of stone
that ran athwart the hill, rebuffed
the eye, but mind took in
traverse and ascent to the top.

As by his own heart muscle, his being
committed to the blank rectangle
'the incarnation of the world.'

Pen to paper: to Ambroise Vollard.
I work with dour determination,
will not give up. This day I caught
glimmerings of the Promised Land.
Will I, like the great Hebrew Chieftan,
never win to it? May I yet penetrate
its bounds? Why only now?
Why so late? I progress – but little.
Why so painfully? My art demands
pursuit of the single way, knowledge
of essential shapes written in nature.
Pen to paper: to Louis Arenches.
My realisation in art? – I think
I attain it more and more – with difficulty.
I have the strong experience of nature,
essential basis on which rests
the grandeur and beauty of all work to come.
Pen to paper: to Emile Bernard.
Forgive me. I repeat my telling you here.
You serve nature by the cylinder, sphere,
the cone, everything in the right perspective
so each side of object or plane directs
towards a central point. Lines parallel
to horizon stretch our, or to put it
quite another way, yields the spectacle.
Pater Omnipotens Aeterne Deus
displays before our eyes. Lines
perpendicular to the horizon give
profundity. Nature for us, humans,
is deeper than surface, so we must
introduce depth into our light
vibrations, reds and yellows and some blues.
so we may feel the sensations of air.

Again the old man went his way – break fast,
studio, work, sustenance, sojourn
to the appointed place. The heat breathless.
'Earth, lay out my body. Rocks,
Crush my corpse!' I would cry out:

'O house of the dead, receive me living!'
Gone. Forty years, Cézanne, the poet,
gone. **Une Terrible Histoire**, 'and the gap
between what is on the page and
what I feel then, feel now, the gap,
that which the brain tells, what
earth, stone-mountain, rock, sky,
tell, and this old hand would utter
on the page of canvas, yet there.'
Still I pursue. Pursue for I am
pursued: seek for I am sought.
'My dear Paul, it is too hot, not
an air to breathe. Even so nature
presents itself to this painter
clearer than before, ever. It
spreads itself before my senses,
yet I cannot win its intensity,
cannot claim for brush and paint
that magnificence that works within
me.' 'My dear Paul, near four o'clock:
there is no air at all. The heat. Heat,
oppresses my brain. I cannot think.
I live in a void. Still I must paint.'
He stares at Mountain and canvas,
canvas and mountain, the moment of
daring, of contact postponed, then
the beginning tortuous with darkest colour,
then layer upon layer, and spread
a little beyond, and then extending
the colours one atop the others, then
move to a new centre, and the same process,
but the centres run counter to each other,
even as in him counters meet, the engagement
a dialogue with self, but bred
of the sensation of the mountain,
weathered, worn, fulfilled in light and dark.
Contraries meet, dissension about him, in him,
and he goes to the mountain.
'Dear Paul, I continue my work
at 4.30am. After 8 I cannot.'
That day in the morning light
it spoke joyously to him.
Even the rocks bathed in sunlight.

Eyes and heart in that new air
lit every fold and convolution
of stony seam, boulder, cliff-face.
Trees, pine and olive, brightened
that day. 'They wait for my brush.
The scene prepares itself for me,
will vanish. Perhaps I catch something.
Despite my weakness I am part of
this massive power, of this mass
that looks at me, has been there,
stays there, compels this veined hand.
Fearful, yet I am enlarged. I am
invaded by the energies of the mountain.'
We look on the rectangle of canvas,
are part of what he has uncovered,
humbled, we receive an essence:
but no, he will not have it so.
'Dear Bernard, my cerebral disturbance,
so great, so confused, I am,
I fear for my frail reason.' Doubts.
Still, will the unchanging provider
of the changing scene, shape, colour, line
allow him 'to set down in my time, that
which tells the tale beyond telling
in words. Will the wilderness of stone
and hill speak to me again?' It is
late afternoon. Another tale is told.
Pitched, we are, into the wide scape,
thrust into, and beyond the pines,
farms, buildings, roads, all transformed.
A weight of blocks of colour, but stabs,
demand attention. Given, but sense and
brain leap to the charge – the touch is lit –
Sainte Victoire – paint tells of tumult:
skies hurtle, burst with life-force –
this is cosmic talk. He is lifted up,
on a high: 'I believe I am impenetrable.'
He will return to Les Lauves. There
he looks no higher than flowers.
In the beam of his eye they offer
all hues – Spring, Summer, Autumn,
Winter. Earth substance, form of flower,
bulk of tree dismissed. He seeks,

gives us the moment of efflorescence.
It is a dialogue of colours. They talk
each to other, agree, disagree,
argue in silent conversation,
form a new union accepting difference.
Be silent with them. A sea of peace
holds him at the last touch of brush.
Monday, October 15 at Les Lauves,
a day of storm, thunder, skies
rent by lightning. He has walked.
An old man stands in the rain.
Hour upon hour it falls: will pass.
Skies will clear, and again
another dawn will break, colours
will flow in sky ways, green
to light-blue, for lark song.
It is a new awakening and he
there to transmit it, to transmute
the common miracle on a white sheet.
Two men find him all unknowing,
return him on their laundry cart,
home. The body is hard to lift
on to the bed. He is still. He sleeps.
Tuesday, October 16. At dawn
he goes down to the small garden
where in Summer he had begun
to paint Vallier the gardener,
as he sat under the lime-tree,
white beard, straw hat on head,
half-asleep, he looked old. He'd
done him in oils, then a solid man.
Now in water-colours he shared
the transience of blossom on the bough.
The dialogue of brush with hill,
brush with earth's fruits, is ended.

> *When he painted a mountain*
> *he painted an apple.*
> *When he painted an apple*
> *he painted a mountain.*

Velazquez

At the Edinburgh International Festival

He turned the searchlight of his mind
upon each and every object equally,
persons or things as if each in its
difference, might through the precision
of line and paint, each weighed in the
balance of a mind, would yield
final truth, each equally capable of
telling the tale that words
could not articulate, telling
in the silence of the canvas –
the egg, the water in the glass,
the gourd, the features of the old
woman, the boy, the seller of water,[33]
water of life he sold – that
crystalline freshness was his
to sell, to sell that which was
beyond price –
O SANCTUS SANCTUS SANCTUS
he heard the silent talk of the
star, and it became humanity.

For the begetter, Michael Clarke, of the Exhibition, 'Velazquez in Seville'
at the National Gallery of Scotland, August 1996

CREATURES

Lost

Black labrador retriever
answers to the name of Swimmer

Over the wall the leap was difficult,
awkward, more a scramble, managed
with the soft belly moulding to the stone.
Left by his master with a friend,
after much travel away from earth's smells,
from cabbage, rhubarb, decaying fungus at the gate,
leather, horse-dung, peat moor, whiff of gunshot,
brown burn, springy heather underfoot, from
sweet green grass, the wide strath, river, loch,
locked in a walled yard smelling of fish,
his kennel once a kiln for smoking haddock,
he barked till dark. At night the foghorn
boomed from the cliff. He howled back. Morning.
Down through the steep, twisting street he ran.
There was no doubting the way to the water.
'Fa echts ee?' spiered Jeems the fisherman
baiting the great lines for his motor-boat:
'Thon's a richt blackie', as the dog hurried by,
slipping soft-footed over the moist pebbles,
then on with a bound to the launching pier,
and raced to a halt at the end. Gulls flew up
in a flurry about him. He sniffed the sea air.
It told tales unheard by him, but known
from his unknown past in traces on the brain,
buried memories waiting on the place, time,
the event, for transmission to nerves, to muscle, to act.
The acts in Labrador were for survival. In winter
the ground is iron. Along the irregular
coast-line, serrated skerries, towering cliffs
threatened the small craft of the fishermen,
colonists of the indented bays. In Summer, cod
and haddock soused in brine, hung on frames
in the open air to dry to be held for winter.
Survival required co-operation. To the North
Eskimos made huskies their agents for transport.

Fishermen on the Atlantic's face found allies
in dogs, strong and sinuous swimmers,
accurate, gentle-mouthed they took back
to the boats cod and haddock, even sea-trout
unmarked, through the wash and buffet of water.
They took the name of their place abroad – Labrador.
A boy with all the force he could, from the pier,
threw a stick out to sea. 'Get it! Go! Get it!'
Dog launched himself. The swell was slow, easy.
He was part of the heaving mass, yielding to it,
it yielding to him, salt sea lifted him up, buoyant.
Once, long time back, a child, girl, Morag,
slipped from the river bank to the Spey.
In a moment he was at her, held her clothes,
bunched, face above water, just, with difficulty,
pushed hard against the stream to outstretched hands.
'Swimmer', she called him. So baptised the name stuck.
The stick offered itself to his jaws. But deep beneath
over the rocky sea-floor a shadow, a swift shape
that carried a command. Here was fish.
The stick floated free. He dived.
In Labrador the sea men knew the flow
and drag of currents, the force of seas
in narrow rents the boats must risk
to win the open sea, knew when to, when
not to, crew boats, men and dogs to hunt.
Boys on the shores of Scottish waters dive
into the breaking wave, giving their bodies
to the undertow, hold breath till sudden
the dynamic fails. Freed they burst surface
into generous air. They know where force
is spent, know too that the calm surface far out
does not disclose below the penetrating race that
holds and brings all caught to the blind depths.
From the pier he saw dog seize the stick,
saw it float free. No more.

Spiered the man: 'Fa echts ee?' 'Nae man has me,
but the shavie watters o the cauld North Sea.'

Koala

At Cleland National Park, South Australia

I
Very slowly he moved with sleep
in his drink-sodden eyes
about the trunk. His position
of backside to me, perhaps,
was not intended as insult,
but not, not a camera shot.

Position reversed – cradled
between tree-arm and trunk,
he is looking at me,
so I flatter myself till
I observe the eyes are closed.

Still the relaxed poise suggests,
or allows for, the acceptance
of another's presence,
or was he just bored
with the whole human race?

II
Without a 'by your leave' or 'may I',
the guide/presenter of the show
plants the creature on my chest.
The tourists click their cameras,
and 'Doesn't he love the dear old man!'

No hint of love or hate, but
indifferently the mammal's claws
are penetrating to my skin.
Am I being signalled that
he and his kin belong
with the dark people
who did not welcome our coming?

Rebuke

There was bread left over
at breakfast, a heel of brown bread,
and I broke it and put it on the stone
ledge at the window: and sparrows came,
a blackbird and a black-capped tit,
and it all went quickly.

And the next morning I did the same,
and it went quickly. Then
the bitter wind came and I kept
the window tight-shut, and a sparrow,
one sparrow, sat on a bush by the window
and cursed me in cheeps. So

I put out more bread, and its friends came
and munched and munched and munched,
and the next day the wind blew colder,
and I kept shut the window;
and the cheeping and cheepering went on.
Why should I fear a sparrow's rebuke
when Sarajevo weeps its eyes out?

Repentance

Now I am making a brown parcel
of all my tomorrows, each one a song
(but of how many I do not know)
to put on the ledge for the cheeping sparrows.

I could guess them, yet still would not know
how to deal with my stained futures.
Sparrows know how to treat
each moment of the day.

In the peek of an eye,
in the flirt of a wing,
in the peck of a beak
in the dust – they know
a meal from a mote.

Haiku Envoi

The sea trembles – voiceless.
It is the rare moment
when a word is sought.

Today Tomorrow
Haikus and Other New Poems

Selected Haikus

For William Soutar (poet)

As a bird
the spirit of the poet rises
from the ashes of despair

Haiku for E.

Glorious this North dawn
I cannot look on it.
My love is not here

25 Warriston Cres.

Night: I come back
to this empty house. My poems
look at me with cold eyes

A Modest Proposal

To exercise power engrave
in stone: to show wisdom
write in sand

Discovery

Who am I? Discover!
I am a child
disguised as an old old man

Laughter

Laughter in the eyes
of the sage. I asked what
it meant. He said laughter

Lucina

Door bolted, windows shuttered
I hear her laughter
in the Spring wind

Burdens

'carry your bags?'
No bags. I journey
carrying the luggage of life

Candles

'Quick, quick' said the bird
'the white candles are lit
on the great chestnut tree.'

5am 24 July 1998
This dawn I awoke with–

The Master said,
'the greatest miracle is
to turn wounds into mercies'

2000

In 1898 Rilke wrote 'Ich lebe grad, da das Jahrhundert geht'

There is a new page to be turned.[34]
In this now, as was, and maybe, tomorrow
we would have a clean page, bright,
shining, not smudged or stained as we
humans scuttle about our businesses,
as if the great sky-scheme that operates
on us, belonged to us, would even,
come time, do our will, but
the vanishing point is reached for one,
always for one, no matter the multitude
of deaths; yet what containment of
stars and sun and moon and planetary
adjuncts in the homeliness of this head.
Is not that miracle enough as the mental
skyship proposes new voyages? But the old
cruelties, terrors, greeds, hates renew themselves
in the amplitude of our abilities to kill.
Still, still there is a delicate logic of hope
heard only by the solitary.

Today Tomorrow

When I saw you on my doorstep
I was in danger of being happy
while cruelty and misery possessed
this globe. To the blind politicians
killing was an acceptable mode
of life in circumstances of necessity,
dressed up, of course, in special words:
'We act to save the nation: a just war:
Our bombs precision bombs, selective:
the tyrant's forces broken, in disarray.
We finished him off. The burned homes
will be replaced, and all will be as was.'
Look at Dubrovnik, the old town by
the Adriatic sea, at peace with itself
Moslem and Catholic sat at café tables
in the street; converse in slow walk
in the street: for this the street was made.
It was enough to be mere human kind,
neighbours were neighbourly; visitors
were at home. War came. They made
a nothing of the street. Ended,
they put it together again as it was.
Picturesque as it was to the eye.
The people were back in place, and sat,
and walked, but in each head death sat
and walked, and when each saw each other,
saw each as if forever other, no longer kin.
They walk the street erect: they talk correct:
the guard is in their tongue:
the guard is in the eye, in case they see and know
that they are kin. O let the children dance
their wayward dance. Around and around
they go, and the dead street floods
with laughter as they pour from thresholds of home.

The Witness

(Written in Australia)

Witness to what? Each page continued
to make its proposals to him that signs
should be put on it, that these
might be picked up by unknown eyes,
an assumption that the deadly rains
had not already destroyed all witnesses.
Certainly there was an impression of continuity –
a cockatoo squawked across the leaden sky,
a snake disturbed the waters that rose
above the floorboards of the room.
But no planes, no sounds of the
combustion engine to comfort. Of that solace
the accompaniment to the routine engagements
which had made civilisation possible,
nothing. No receiver of signs, then no
necessity. Yet perhaps as that last bird
sped between the boughs uttering harsh cries,
as the snake's body looped and unlooped
in muddy waters there was the last requirement
to find that impossible speech which sang
of the creation that was.
                   In the gathering dark
of that upper room he looked out
at the swaying, cracking branches. Sound,
movement, possibly a twinkle in the gum's leaves,
then in the perceiver, light in the eyes.
The sweet word rolled from the tongue:
Light. Light. Light.

L' Annunciazione

Beato Angelico, San Marco

The illusion could hardly be
more distant from the facts,
the arrival of the final miracle.
In some rough hut or cave,
stable, the usual pain and he
emerges bloody, squalling
into this world. What if
the truth was in the illusion,
and out of our time the universe
that casually threw this planet
presents the contradiction.

Lucina — to the Lighthouse![35]

Fraser o Saltoun biggit the shut face
o Kinnaird Castle agin the force o seas.
This wis his prood hame. Wun an watters
brak boats an men on the rocks.
Ae Fraser chiel socht mair comfort
for hame. Then for the safe bein
o a sea wanderers there thrust up
Kinnaird Lichthoose tooer. Noo stan
at the tap an look on the great watters
an lift. Lat yer een be blint
i the flash o the fite breakers,
an dark i the deep sea, as did
Lucina heich abune the tide race
an took to hersel that wild world's embrace.

Returning to the Broch[36]

In Memoriam Robert Bruce (1910–99)

The place of your birth and growing-up
is never the same on return.
In the beginning God made it for ever.
The South Church stands bright
in morning sun. Even the Central School
in its grey granite sparkles. Remember
the cold rock pools at low tide, providers
of partans,[37] greenbacks,[38] cumpers,[39] flukes[40]
destined for the blue pail in the hand.
I would pour them back in the water
in that time, and again I am in that time
now and no storm raves in my forever.
Now there is another present by me and he
would have them back in their places
one at a time, for he would know
what happened to each, and why?
They told me – he is your brother.
He is the one who would know for sure.
Yet all to me was wonder and strange,
and he, child, barely into his teens
said 'There is no God. I am an atheist,'
And no-one paid much attention and I,
devout in ice-cream, am running
and jumping, and leap so long, so high,
I am ten minutes in air before
I found touch down. 'Rubbish' said my brother
and ran fast through the years but
deliberately, stopped, briefly as he met
Hegel (Plato was always with him). When
in the middle years of the 'dismal science'
and our people broken – Marx thrust
his solution upon him. Robert sent
Das Kapital to our father, who read it,
expounded it to the makers of barrels
as they thundered the iron hoops[41] about
wooden staves as small fires of shavings
glowed, encircled by barrels to hold herring.
They, coopers, were not enamoured
of his presentation. 'This' he said 'was
matter for debate.' And so it was and

always at the dinner-table – mid-day dinner.
I return. I see great skies, terrible seas.
Upon the retina of the brain, printed,
a boy, naked, is swept in white water
raging round a rocky point. He would
hold to the stone, but the back-wash
has him. Gone, till the forward power
of water again and again sweeps up
the body. 'Run' bawled Robert 'I'll run
for help.' I stay and watch a drowning.
This I store from time long past.
We return to the table to debate.
By the way he had met Confucius:
A point of beginning, but you
cannot be with Confucius without
being at one with his talk. So
he is there, and with Buddha,
far from the appetites of the West,
where nothing is allowed just to be
itself, where place and the hand that put
on the writing surface Taoism, Buddhism,
Zen, Basho travelling with his pack of Haikus –
he was there and in the tongue of
Canton, Mandarin, Hokkien, Hakka,
to be applied as suited, and he
half-blind, but seeing a continuum,
discovering an essence, like the bee
to the flower, not one kind of flower,
to make the sweetness of honey,
so he would return, perhaps, not
knowing why, to that rugged source
the Broch, to that place, which,
as child he made his first rejection
in four words: 'I am an atheist'.[42]
Now half-blind, then blind, he
returned with two words: the Christ.

This day, 2 October 1999,
I stand in Kirkton Kirkyard amongst
the bones of my ancestors and think
of the brave spirit of Robert.

Written as at the grave of Robert Bruce

The Stones of the Arch

A reconsideration of the poem 'A Gateway to the Sea' (1950)

Once, I thought, once these stones are named,
cut, dressed given their place, one upon one
to form the arch of grey sandstone (now sable)
that they had entered into a compact with man –
they were on our side, accomplices in our order
accepting the verdict of human history,
as if they never were what once they had been,
nor would return to that incomprehensible no-time,
whose time we cannot tell or keep, nor measure
by the pulse. It is pretence to count light years.
Without consciousness they make no light,
no sound in their passage. Words cannot reach them.
Whose Word is theirs? What logic do they promulgate?
When all the words are burst and the silver stars
are stones and the stones dissolve to dust,
as is our dissolution, and we have no time to keep
and the knowledge to which we should aspire,
abdicating the self, is that we know nothing.
The stone face of this arch deceives.
It does not belong to us. It belongs
to the wildness of the air and water,
to that other where there is no word for love.
Let us then unlabel these stones.
Let the sea swallow them.
Let them be with that other universe
where no time is kept.
In the transparent moment of unknowing
will we be entered by the other,
or will the other receive us?

The Eye

In Memoriam Tadeusz Kantor[43]

Zalisniete szurkiem przylepione plastrem
'Held together by string and sticking plaster'

He towered – a ruined tower – his wear
formal, yet not, not to be expected, nor
appropriate for the acolyte of a thespian temple –
these tails, white-starched front, white bow-tie,
sought the perfection of the servile order,
one of those who waited at the table,
napkin on forearm at the ready, but
stained, perfection failed, the gear creased,
rumpled, hung on the huge frame as if
off the peg, having been occupied by another.
Only the indifferent stare, the pâpier-maché
feature matched that ultimate stereotype
from which had drained the blood of being.
Now in the semi-dark with the sensation
of the sweetness of milled grain in the nostrils
doubt crept in as to whether I was in the right place
for a performance. I had fumbled at a latch,
stumbled through the small door inset in the great door
hung, that once would slide aside with thump and rumble
and out would come two dray horses jingling into day,
their long lorry laden with bag upon bag upon bag
of flour. On their way with the provision of bread
for the city they would pass, as I had done,
the graveyard with the bones of the poet,
Donnchadh Ban Mac an t-Saoir,[44] and the kirk
of the Grey Friars. The small door was for human entry.
As the waiter-warder took my ticket, his presence,
its unassailable confidence, presuming I had no option,
I had been called as witness, took possession.
No word spoken; he took me along the white-walled
passage. Candle-lit it played his enormous shadow
as on a screen, and mine diminished, wavering,
without substantial existence. A sudden right turn
and a humming rose and fell from occupants unseen.
Led to the side of the hall, placed on a chair
cane (precarious) at a small, round table for one,
white (stained) tablecloth, the circumstance
began to disclose itself, I was at a small-paned

window, where still on the sills flour
reminders of the previous occupation: but
now others seated, similarly against the wall
of the long dimly lit rectangular hall,
waited expectant, as they say, for the curtain
to rise, though there was none, and the performance
– activity rather – had begun, might have
been going on for hours: now nightfall,
possibly since day broke – or earlier. Certainly
we were not encouraged to view: the players
went on with their own business while a select few
of us, spectators, were served with black coffee.
One waiter approached a kilted spectator,
then hastily withdrew the offer, to which the head waiter
nodded his assent. As if in imitation of him
these members of the tribe resembled the ashen face,
height, demeanour, and in dress the stained napkins
held precisely above the wrists, rings on pink hands.
I was honoured by the offer of coffee. Anxious to see
the stage, my view blocked by the black back,
I dared not say 'no'. We were to be contained,
marginalised, silenced, while about and about
an agitated multitude went about their business.
This was the show. Yet each heedless of us,
nothing for us, implacable in the pursuit
of what each must do, one jerking the neck,
his stare following the long irregular crack
on the white-washed wall, switching his gaze
to the holes in the ceiling and the rotting beams,
'House of God,' his lips whisper, then the shout:
'Dead, dead, dead, dead'. By him stands tall top-hat,
black coat, black gloves, shining black shoes,
he, necrophagous, anticipating an event. The typist,
perched high on a threelegged stool, her bony fingers
reach to the antique spider-like typewriter
higher on a plinth. The recording angel types: 'Dead'
in large capitals centred on A-4 paper.
She holds the page aloft for all to see.
No-one appears to heed, but the low murmur
heard on entering rises again, a continuum
of sound: at first apparently a general moaning,
then the recognition of intoning, a response,
possibly to the word exhibited, arriving in the ear

as the articulated sounding of a quiet sea.
Momentarily the multiplicity of diverse activities,
so great it could be imagined the genus
of every necessary work was present,
and many to little purpose (to the accompaniment
of gossiping, quarrelling, whispering, shouting,
cursing, laughing, weeping, grinding the teeth,
munching, retching, belching, farting and other
humanities) **CEASED**. The buzz of being stilled.
And in the moment of petrifaction, as they froze
in their attitudes – was it possible to recognise
the confusion concealed an order? There were present
the preparers for life – the mid-wife with the tools
of her trade, a steaming kettle, towels, bandages,
the masked surgeon, and the accompanists of ending,
the black pall-bearers, the white collar with blood-red
HOPE on it: and between, the sowers of seed, the bakers
of bread, the kind killers of meat-for-food, the fishers,
caught at an angle as the swell lifts the boat,
the brick-layers, makers of walls to protect and divide,
the knitters (droppers of stitches for death) whose ball
of wool ran from them over the lip of the stage
into the channel that ran, a dark strip, to separate
them, the actors from us, who sat, yet had a part
(one whispered secretly forbidden knowledge) to play.
And unseen, the subterranean miners – child, woman, man –
nor heard their beating from their confined pasts,
rock or coal-face or abstract void, deaf to their
stunned blows that rang too deep for hearing,
yet in that pause so close we were to being,
the breathing of generations permeated mass, chilled
the air about us, and we would have shut our ears
and put our hands to the candle-flame for warmth
but that we too were transfixed: yet now know
we stood in that time, and from that moment of prescience
knew, without a word, each of us contained centuries,
and that each life could not be quantified.
This no more than the most momentary glimpse
of time beyond accountability. In this society
they knew their place. Function, hierarchy prevailed,
fundamental needs met. So the long trestled table
centred, white table cloth provided for the eaters,
heads above table level champed their jaws,

slurped their drink, obedient, 'leave no crumbs'
be exemplars to all as in time they chewed,
swallowed, digested, while at the ready
for them the plates replenished, the cup
filled again and again. Yet this was the day
of INTERRUPTION.[45] On the white-sheeted table
lay what had been a being. There was an
ambiguity about the corpse. The bulk suggested
male, well-clad, yet the pink plastic mould
with undisputed breasts marked it female.
She was our brother or sister, kin by being
human. She stared glass-eyed upwards
to the sentinel cameras recording the scene,
CCTV, for the guardians, police only, permanent
fixtures until this moment for each of the players
and each member of the audience, as far as one knows
(for who am I to presume that the great staring eye
was there, central in my (our) experience, replacing
the architected ceiling). Further if I closed my eyes
it burned through the lids. It must be, must be,
personal to each, perhaps to me alone. We were not
suspects; we were the convicted. Whomsoever entered,
whomsoever left, it moved with their movement. Here
was a convention outwith the agreed convention of
murder. Our rulers, politicians, never murdered. We
made weapons of mass destruction. We sold them
to another. Blood was not on our hands. We had
appropriate categories for the disposal of others.
This killing, the body associated with food,
was nauseous. The manual of instruction
on inappropriate behaviour made no comment.
A place had to be found for it, acceptable to
the public imagination. At the discovery of
the deceased – the clinical term is necessary
for the disposal of feeling – all were transfixed.
Yet not by the decaying matter on the table,
a single act – the sudden, silent presence
of The Eye disposed of in a moment
the fabric of laws, customs, above all
agreed modes of expression which put a gloss
on acts which might be regarded as inappropriate
to the sustainment of our culture. We had thought
we had absorbed into that nexus which finally

bonded us all ways and means of civilised living,
had contained griefs by appropriate rituals, given,
at least virtual reality to the stoppage of death,
keyed processes from our computer which diminished
the naked sensation of the violence of nature,
and enacted on screens terrifying cruelties, assaults
on persons, swindlings and lyings, blasphemies
and obscenities, so that we no longer knew them
for what they were: and here was something done
out of place and out of our scale of time.
That arrest of power, which we knew, which
temporarily held our world in suspense,
was simply explained as climax to
our death ritual, but over the *Interruption*
our computers seemed to have no control.
What, what, what had happened? Had
all the computers on this planet
CRASHED? Then, as the cant phrase
has it – we were back to square 1.

So, back to a beginning. Which?
'Let there be light' There was a little left.
Once upon a time there were dawns
of good lineage. Homer had watched
'*the rosy-fingered dawn*' presage
a new day with the clamour of birds.
Still we had a little, ashen as from
the dying faces of our black-clad monitors.
Like the light from carbyde flairs it spread
to every face in the incoming tide of dark.
Yet beyond the North-East corner of
the Play Pen rectangle a different illumination,
an old man warms his hands at glowing coals
of his brazier. He is the Nightwatchman.
In view of the survey of the scene by CCTV
his function was, presumably, superfluous,
but they had gone from the sky; The EYE[46]
had taken over, but not him. He occupied
an area between the stage and audience.
Seated, though he stared at the fire, his gaze
was inward. On the back of his chair in
bold black letters were the initials: T. K.
The chair was extraordinarily like C. B. de Mille's

on the set for a Biblical epic though the shape
of the man, small, slim, black-bearded was
singularly unlike that master of the grand.
He got to his feet with ease, boarded
the Play Pen, and made towards the body.
He had, apparently, assistants who proceeded
to lift it from the table, placing it with care
in a bath unnoticed by spectators
for it was obscured by the general hub-bub
as the actors bobbed up and down in their
efforts to get notice taken of them which
might further their careers. Now in the suspense
of activity not only did the white enamel of the
bath shine out, but also a red liquid, occupying
about three-quarters of the bath, allowing
the naked body of a young woman to create
displacement of the liquid without a single
drop of spillage. It was as if decency had returned
to the scene. This was the way our people
wanted it to be, and so it was real. Job done.
The troupe followed the Master, standing attentive
in a single line off-stage, forming a kind of
guard of honour, awaiting the arrival of a person
of great distinction – a football manager, a bishop,
a multi-millionaire, pop-star – all comforters of our times.
Gradually the terrible rigidity of the company
relaxed. The terror was taken from them.
The effulgence of The Eye weakened, and even
as it was disappearing from the firmament
a figure was seen threading its way through
the multitude. They showed no surprise
at the approach of the tall, slim man
in cape and deer-stalker hat. Holmes
took up his position near the head of
the woman in the bath, produced
a magnifying glass, and began to study
the body in detail. He entered his observations
in a note-book. The Nightwatchman had waited
to see if his repair was effective, if it was
consonant with the condition of virtual reality,
the trauma, which was normality for our society.
Within these terms we were made whole again.
At a sign his party shambled along the aisle.

I had not noticed that each carried an instrument.
The leader, wearing a battered top-hat,
plucked the strings of an Irish banjo, his attention absorbed
in the act. There followed, tripping, a dark-haired girl,
touching with her stick a triangle. Behind her a fat
bald man hit with force a bass drum. A boy played
a Jew's harp. Last in the procession, the dancer
her movements, sinuous, womanly, she shook
and banged a tambourine: her dress rainbow rich
in colours of the East. Pinned to it, centred
at her breast, a Burnett rose hinted a loyalty
other than India. Yet no sound was heard[47]
from dancer or from players, from beat
of drum to pipe of flute. It was as if
we had no place, no home in this
their mode of life: our ears too gross.
Their music drawn from springs and airier
skies than we could know. Earth
spoke to them with a different tongue.
Estragon and Vladimir would have heard it.
Then came the Master, Nightwatchman, T.K.
Bound for elsewhere he carried baton and bag.
Passages were now dark, yet enough light to see
heaps of black clothing, white shirts, cuff-links,
discards of those who minded us. But what
identity was theirs now, refugees from this planet?
Afterwards I recollected I had heard the Master
mumble to himself in a language I did not know:
'Held together by string and sticking plaster!'

Happenings in back-gardens by the Water of Leith

The Fox and Lucina

So long they looked it was as if eternity
had entered in our mortal world

One fine Spring morning I looked
upon my patch of rough green grass,
and he was there, sunlit. Rarely
had I seen a creature with such poise
in sleep, for so the animal, brown coat,
with white under-belly, appeared to be,
until I noticed one ear at the ready,
pricked for threat of danger, survival.
I could not move for any movement
of mine was cumbersome against his
most delicate engagement with earth.
Then undisturbed, the visitor was on the wall.
Gone, and I was the poorer for his absence. He
looked in from time to time, but I
was no priority – and then, no more.
He had gone elsewhere, as I discovered
as I told, with some small boast, Lucina,
(who is as fair as is her name). 'My fox,'
she said. More orderly than mine, he preferred
her green place with the stream running by.
No posture of sleep for him. He
looked around, alert, took in all.
One day she went to the open door.
He rose to his feet. He did not go away.
He looked at her and she at him for long.
There was no fear nor hating
in his eyes, and no enmity in her,
for she knew his beauty honoured
the earth they shared.

The Singing of the Foxes

Another note for John Bellany

Sudden, in the night a voice
calls, no more than a call, but
sustained, the pitch never lost,
true to the single note, but who?
and why? It came, it seemed,
across the stream, artless
as a child, yet accomplished
beyond childhood's reach. A voice
from a creation other than human
called and called and called.

Time past I looked on the figuration
of Velazquez and on the great fresco,
The Effects of Good Government,
by Ambrogio Lorenzetti in the
Palazzo Pubblico in Siena and each
told the same tale of the indisputable
meaning of life. Now the energies
of the universe howl in our darknesses
and we say 'why? why? why?'
and no answer is at hand, only
the killing rains, the desert out there
and in the mind; the earth quakes.
Yet, you put the brush to canvas
with such assurance as if
there was still meaning in life
somewhere around. The rains[48]
had killed the land which for
hundreds of years the people
of the land had made grow food
now killed them, sent people,
precarious, to climb trees
for life's sake. One woman*
gave birth in a tree: the child
survived. Then uncaring nature
carried death on its own, but we
for greed, for gain carried death
for others. Some carry death,
death in themselves, and would
would expel it as righteousness

* During the Mozambique flood of 2000.

to whom, they thought had no truth
in them but *they* had the whole
truth and nothing but the truth,
and so in their pride committed
a blasphemy, and the disease
spread through all our kind.
Now, they kill the spirit of love.
Now deaf to all but the self
we kill the body as never before.
Sudden, you picked up the brush
and this *auld warld was by wi,*
and a new world was before us
fresh, clear and without stain,
and each house stood as if
the dressed stones were made
with love. Sky and waters shone
as if they could be no other.
The chemistry of paint became
the chemistry of love. Nothing
had changed. The matière was
the same as ever. Folk went about
their business as ever. A housewife
sloshed her windows from a pail.
A fisherman painted his boat,
another made repairs, two talked,
but the beam of the mind at the
first touch of brush translated all.
As the silent images grew, translucent,
we recognised original innocence –
the artist the honoured transmitter
of what lay waiting for discovery.

This night I heard the little foxes,
their soft-pitched mellow voices sing,
innocent as childhood. One voice first.
She calls and calls, until distant another
calls. She outlasts all others, sustains
the pitch exact until the call dies
in the moonlight. They came here
from the graveyard over the stream,
past Natasha's house, past Deborah's,
past Francesca's, past Gloria's house –
all have given hostages to fortune.

They are asleep. I listen to voices
from the other kingdom. They talk
to others of their kind in kindness.
'I am here – come, come' or
'I come to you.' They project their kind
into the future. They act in the confidence
that the future is theirs: the matter is not
for debate. It is not noted in the minutes.
We are noted in the minutes. When registered,
the State allows we exist. Notation is our trade
tapped on paper or tapped. As never before
we discover depth and height. We break through
visible barriers, note the great abstracts
in ever more embracing equations.
The data-base renews our confidence
in our ability to record all phenomena.
All will be well as long as (they say)
as long as mind abstracts itself from
being. Now we have begat immediate
communication but what is communicated?
We have shrunken the world to be closer
to all, only to be further away.
The little foxes call in the dark.
I hear them as the generations
heard them, and their message is
'We are as we were. Listen, for
if Nature is not heeded you are
the endangered species.' Out
of the fragmented being comes
the fragmented self: it divides
and hates; yet the singer sings
to no purpose, but because
she must and all who can hear
are at one with the singer
and the maker of songs
and the maker of images
who have taken to themselves
the cruelties of this world
and from them made a new thing.
The blood-hungry fox sings a new song.

The Picture

Homage to Hisashi Momose,
who makes permanent the moment

Sometimes one sees a painting
in an Exhibition. You cannot pass it
and move to the next and next –
for you are held in its stillness.
Lift your eyes from it and move
down the stairs and a new beauty
is in their simplicity. You have heard
the earth has exploded, but that
is in another place. Step outside
and the Square is right for what
it is meant to be, its formality
is what good Squares must have.
Even the blue of the sky is tempered.
There must be a deal of virtue around,
but who played that card? Was it
the painter, or the conjunction of the
right companion preparing the way
to look at the product of a delicate hand.

How to Hang a Big Picture

For Sue and Mike Adler

First make up your mind to get married
to the right person, otherwise no matter
what you do it will remain askew.
Then engage a Professor of the History
of Art, who will apply herself to right angles,
while a Master of the History of Fine Art
applies himself to left angles. Add in
the artist, one bald antiquity, plus
one bustling child, as spectators,
critics, applauders, loungers on sofa,
and all is set for the containment of form,
and this form is alive with creation –
snake-shapes, box-shapes, dice-shapes,
running lines, jumping dots, spaces,
interrupted by weighty components

that float in a sky, high – all held
together, awaiting the great uplift.
DONE. Hold breath. It stays on wall.
When the house is asleep each
pulsing piece slips from its picture
place and dances silent on the floor.
Morning. Two stare at the painting.
It is ringed with happiness.

*Translation of above: I shall be happy to attend the Warriston
celebration of your wedding on Saturday, 16 October*

Barbara Visits my Bookshelves

The books had gone wild, didn't like
their categories on the shelf. They
jostled, pushed their neighbours around –
easy for hardbacks; flexis had a bad time,
some squeezed out were catapulted, carpeted.
All fought for top place in his mind.
Turmoil was on the floor, sheets of poems
got shabby treatment; no decency in them,
scattering, whispering, cutting remarks
everywhere. All blamed him for disorder.
'It was, of course, his mind.' Barbara
settled to the job, first sobered them up.
Those on the shelves slouched, supported
each other, drunken, having lost
their sense of gravity. Then the floor poems
found themselves picked up, dusted down,
smoothed, sorted into piles, ordered into files.
Now one might believe in an ordered universe.
'Who created the disorder?' Not him, he offered
no apology. 'It was them that did it, them
that made a hole in the sky.' He 'suicidal
business-man' could not afford to put it right.
They done it for sure with their emissions.
I'm asking Barbara to put them right.

Epistle to David

At Rosebank, Helensburgh

You set me at the computer,
already set for my first touch.
Instruction. Write. But what?
A white mist settles on the house.
Nothing meets the eye: no
weeping ash, no green grass,
no rhododendron's pink,
no gean white, no dyke beyond,
no Firth of Clyde. Could touch
put words to paper in this
blank vacuum? Write, and
the finger of the mind penetrates,
holds together this moment
and time past. All computed.
One white sheet of ice stretches
the Firth, smothers rock and earth.
Still, utterly still, silent. No tread
of foot, no ear to hear, so no
sound, no name Clyde. It is
a still – so human eye might –
might witness. The mental eye
reports it moves. In this
no time the ice mass moved.
In such matters we had no part.
But walk down the broad stairs
of this house: stand between
its pillars at the entrance. Let
it remember its dream. The
banks of the Clyde beckoned
to the merchant Princes, who
built mansions and marinas,
where yuccas prospered
in the Scottish air. All was
mildness. Propriety ruled.
Croquet flourished on the lawns.
Business was the sleight
of hand that conjured
landau, paddle boat, parasols,
afternoon teas, dinner at seven,
top hats, stays – the Victorian heaven.

Gone. But the broad river ran strong,
carried the wealth of nations,
called for, and got, men devout
in making vessels, applying brawn
and brain to the job, each vessel
to be right for its job, so invention
prospered, so Bell's *S.S. Comet*. Here
was the thrust of life. And Glasgow went
doon the wa'er. Engines churned,
clanged, barrels of beer and bands
aboard the *Waverley* as it sailed,
steamed its daily dream, swam to
Rothesay, Dunoon and the Kyles,
and not a voice was idle: and
in this house other voices –
the throb of life in the drum,
the shout of life in the voice,
the mellow voice of cello,
and music walks the street
in Helensburgh.

The New Scottish Poetry Library

Dedicated to Malcolm Fraser, architect

First there was its silence. Each true
building has its silence, particular to
itself and purpose. There is a command
to the entrant. 'Wait,' and allow stone
and wood and light to utter soundlessly.
Bypassing the outer ear this keeper
of written thoughts, gave two words
to the hearer – 'limpid clarity'. Once
years and years ago I looked through
the transparence of sea water
of the rock pool to the white micaceous
sand of its floor, across which a small
crab moved its articulated limbs to
the cover of a strand of wrack at
the pool's edge. The gleam of a
stationary peerie fish despite its sculptured
stillness insisted life was here, and in the tremble
of tide the pink anemone swayed. The wonder
of a world of light – fact and vision one thing –
unasked, presented itself, but here now
the directive to build a new poetry library
was explicit. Here to be contained
was a repository of personal and national
experience in the medium of that
rhythmical concentration of words,
known as poetry: but the concept
of the scholar in semi-dark drawing
light into himself, cherishing the small flame
was not here. The whole stone building
is a response to poetry – a visual poem
in itself. The wild light upon crags and sea
bursts in a blaze through ceiling apertures.
There leaps to the mind a voice singing:
'*Were na my hert licht I would dee.*'
This capsule of light has taken into itself
laughter and the deep grief of Cresseid:
'*Fader, my mirth is gone.*' Light has no weight:
it may be hard, strong, gentle, fierce, kind –
all here, it runs with the flow of stairways:
it gathers in dance groups of children.
This light has the limpid clarity of enlightenment.

City Inscape

Edinburgh. Honeymoon. Afternoon. 26/7/35

Looking across the street from Georgian windows,
between smoke-blackened buildings, I had,
(I thought) an *illusion*, sun-lit cyan-pink cliffs.
Impossible, looked away, hoping something douce,
decent, belonging to this city of good repute,
would replace my mental error, I looked again.
It was there – a vast theatrical backdrop,
but no insubstantial curtain, no mirage.
Rough-shod it arrived. Earthed the Crags,
holding magmatic intrusions, give notice
of a long lodgement, and with the sleeping
carboniferous volcano awaits the show
which history would provide. Geology,
the 'makar' provided for the fortress castle
that topped the black volcano whose
basalt plug broke the ice-flow about
the rock. The drive gouged out, channelled
deep, athwart both sides, leaving on high
the ridge. First folk built about the Castle
a huddle of houses for their safekeeping,
then down the ridge that sprouted closes,
vennels, wynds. So Auld Reekie was made
ready for deeds o' a kinds, nefarious and
the dance of life, ready for the play of Kings
and commoners who wouldna wait
for answers, but, acted, as did Scotland's
King who left the Castle council in haste
to hold to him his fair new wife across the Firth.
He crossed in storm, warned, went on,
but fell to his death from Kinghorn's cliffs.[49]
The pattern of the play was set. Murder,
and Rizzio's music was stilled, and Mary's
King blown to pieces in Kirk o Fields.
Alas poor Queen. Alas the Deacon,[50]
whose contraption didn't save his neck.
Past and present are here about us.
The native rock breaks through
the Castle's stone: and we are bonded
to our human past and to that past
beyond our kenning. Now is needed

some act of that imagination that brings all
together, and this has been done. Suddenly
it seemed it was there – a mediaeval bastion,
fortress, a round as for a defence, intruded
on Chambers Street[51], its curve taken up again
and again on floor after floor in a new great
edifice, till at the top look north and see
the Castle display its power in rounded
battlement, now echoed here. Empty
this building of the artefacts of our history
and still it speaks of Edinburgh. Inside
not confinement but a liberation of space
and light. *The Illusion* is of forms
of such purity of line, bathed in light
as if they had no other function
than to transport the mind. Ascend
and corridors running the length
of the building are visions of vennels,
wynds, closes, lifted by imagination
out of the particulars of stone.
Here new and old are as one. In those
who accept, the pulse of life beats stronger.

The Breaking of Barriers

*These lines were written at the request of Malcolm Mackay as a summary of an ideal for
'Law at Work'. They may also apply to the breaking of the barrier of the Berlin Wall.*

Our tomorrow grows from the bud of today,
would flourish in all who would walk
new ways, not saying 'no' to yesterday
when the seed was planted, yet not bound
to that past, but open to fresh, new airs
that blow down barriers, unite our being
in common humanity. We see anew our selves
in others, others in our selves. Quick,
quick open your heart and mind to all kind.

A Birthday Gift from John Bellany

A painting of the harbour and houses of Port Seton, East Lothian

John

You took my breath away
and gave it back ten times over.
What daylight here!
What dance of light!
caught in a mind that still
could believe meaning, life-giving
meaning, could still be here,
here in your magnanimity,
in the truth of your imagination,
and you send me this great gift.
At least it's given to one who
fifty-eight years ago wrote these
words about another place,
'Did once the sea engulf all here and then
at second thought withdraw to leave
a sea-washed town?'
Sturdy the houses, biggins sea-resistant,
boats hammered sea-worthy –
all bathed in light.
House and boat, sweep of road-way,
bright, alive with sea-borne airs.
It is an air that blew away
each particle of dust,
each human blemish.
It goes about and about and I
am in it, rejoicing in this quick
of life of colour and always the eye
taken up and blown sea-wards.
I leaped in my childhood.
My age has gone: I leap again.

George

Sea Woman

Who reads the Book of the Sea
reads the Book of Life

These eyes have looked on the sea
for long, for long. Read now
in them a cartography of grief
and laughter. She is the home-coming
from chartless waters. Genesis
is in her. She has looked on the sea
and there was no return. Look now
on these eyes and know, caught in the
net of mortality, she looks at us,
the immortal She.

To Eddy at Eighty

Morgan the Master Makar
four linked haikus

In Siena I was
wakened in the night
by the throaty chorus of frogs.

I thought the silence
of the campanile
is far better than that.

Over the town in silence
the beauty of this tall
lady presides.

Now be they short or tall
I am silenced by
the beauty of your poems.

Waiting Room – Leuchars December

For Helen who made a garden

I am at the window –
wintry dried grass in the field.
Through a break in the cloud,
pale-blue sky – a window from earth.

Edwin Muir stood here, waiting
for the train that took him
to his war-time job in Dundee.[52]
His poems – another window.

Now, once again the sky is polluted
by war-planes' emissions and roar.
In summer, from a green bank, blooms
the sculpted, White Burnett rose.

Now

Now is the time for amazement
No angels in this sky.
The blue sings itself.
Daffodils shout their hallelujas.
Seas sing their terrible songs.
The earth-worm snooves in the dark.
Above, new grass trembles.
It is the throb of life.

Tomorrow

Tomorrow
Tomorrow
will be
tomorrow
before I
am ready
for tomorrow
so
let it stay
today.
Moment of a
moment in time.
Blessed be the moment.

G.B. wrote this in the Royal Museum of Scotland while testing a new pen he had purchased in the Museum's shop.

Ed.

The Song of Henry Cockburn[53]

What could be more delightful
within a town? The sea of Bellvue foliage
gilded by the evening sun: the tumult
of blackbird and thrush sending
their morning notes into the blue
of summer air – this was his Edinburgh.
This way he would have it.

'On still nights I have stood, looked
at the prospect from Queen Street
gardens, and listened to
the corncraik's ceaseless rural call.
All Leith Walk was fully set with wood.
No Scotch city so graced with trees.
How can I forget the glory of the scene.'
This is the way he would have it.

But that for money's sake blank
city walls broke off his views.
His war of words struck home.
Still Edinburgh was Edinburgh,
But that his continuum of protest
must end. Lord Cockburn now,
Senator of the College of Justice,
Judge. In silence he must sit
through every city hurt.

But that his human heart prevailed
would do so until his end.
Ayr – his last circuit journey.
After the trial he noted: 'One of the
finest days of this unsurpassed
Spring. The advancing sea insinuating
its clear waters irresistibly, yet gently.
There was no sound – a picture of repose.'
Home – serenity in his ending.

No longer here to mark out right from wrong,
The Cockburn bears the burden of his song.

To Lucina

who, in editing my poems, overpraised them

Know that each time you find
some merit, some small beauty
in a poem written by this hand
it is not of me. Then I stood
out of the light, my shadow
did not intervene. My merit is
I cast no shadow. There was
a moment, as daylight weakened,
this December afternoon: suddenly
you looked up, and the poem became
its self.

Notes

A Song for Scotland (p. 11)
1. 'The dead herring on the living water': a reference to those occasions when the fishermen dumped the herring back into the sea, having considered that the price offered for the catch was inadequate. When this action was repeated by many boats it was done in the hope that the shortage of fish thereby created would result in higher prices at the auction of the following day's catch.

Sea Talk (p. 19)
2. 'being a cranner': eight baskets of herring equalled the measure of one cran. The cranner was an employee of the buyer of the fish who counted the baskets as they were swung from boat to pier. He was responsible for seeing to it that each basket was full to overflowing and for noting that the quality of the fish was similar to what the fisherman had shown to the buyer as a sample of the catch. He also saw to it that the fish were heavily sprinkled with salt before they left the pierhead. He was therefore intimate with both sides of the business, would not be given to sentiment yet was known to express admiration for the honesty and character of the fisherman. The poem is written from a cranner's point of view.

A Man of Inconsequent Build (p. 39)
3. H.G.B. – George Henry Bruce, my father – was head of *A. Bruce and Co.*, the oldest herring-curing firm in the north of Scotland. He had no interest in making money, beyond acquiring the bare necessities of life – food, books, clothes. He is also described in *A Departure*.

Sumburgh Heid (p. 58)
4. The rocky headland at the south of the Shetland Isles. The poem is largely onomatopoeic, being descriptive of the sounds and atmosphere about Sumburgh Head.

Valediction for Henry Moore 1944 (p. 60)
5. The opening of the poem describes one of Henry Moore's shelter drawings.

The Singers (p. 64)
6. The quatrains in Scots describe the fisherman's day and accident. Breakfast consists of porridge and a 'spelding frae the rack'- dried fish (haddock or whiting) taken from the rack on which they were hung. 'ower meat we maun be swack' – over our meat we must be quick; meat in Aberdeenshire refers to food in general.

Fishermen's Cliff Houses (p. 69)
7. This poem was written as a response to Anne Redpath's painting, *Fishermen's Cliff Houses*.

Landscapes and Figures (p. 70)
8. The first section describes an Aberdeenshire landscape. The rest is Holy Isle – Lindesfarne (Northumbria). There is a legend that crows stole the thatch from the roof of St Cuthbert's cottage.

The Island (p. 72)

9.	My grandfather, George Bruce, was one of the earliest herring curers to set up a fishing station in Baltasound.

Aberdeen, the Granite City (p. 76)

10.	'The Assembly Rooms', now known as the Music Hall, was built by Archibald Simpson, Aberdeen's most distinguished architect.

A Pigeon's Feather (p. 101)

11.	On Ember Day, 18 September 1968, after viewing *The Coronation of the Virgin Mary* by Fra Angelico in the Louvre, my wife picked up a pigeon's feather near La Sainte Chapelle.

Chestnut Tree – June 1970 (p. 120)

12.	The date of an earthquake in Peru.

On the Edge – The Broch (p. 199)

13.	'The Broch' – the local name for Fraserburgh.
14.	There were several James Buchans in Mid Street, Inverallochy, hence the substitution of numbers for the name. Gilbert, his son, also came to be known as 7½.
15.	The sight of Mormond Hill from the sea, from a particular angle, gave the skipper the assurance he would get a good run in to Fraserburgh Harbour.
16.	Two reproductions, one of a horse, the other of a deer, were laid out in white stone on Mormond Hill. They were not ancient but Victorian.
17.	'Immemorial', of course. The boy got it wrong, or three was a syllable too many for the rhythms.
18.	In February 1993 I was invited by George Gunn, then Writer-in Residence in Macduff for Banff and Buchan, to present a selection of my poems, and to write one for the first of *The Five Touns Festivals*, which was held in Fraserburgh, my home town. The programme was also sustained by Edwin Morgan. Since the poem was to be performed before a local audience, the episodes and references had to be factually correct, as they are, though there is some exaggeration in the reporting. On leaving my home at 2 Victoria Street, the milk cart became airborne, at least it felt like that. I have to admit too that my grandfather was not present on the occasion, but he did in his nineties, greet all, his walking stick raised, with 'Praise the Lord!'
19.	James Buchan spoke these words in conversation for the Scottish Home Service (Radio) for the BBC.

Ian in the Broch (p. 211)

20.	Having visited Scotland's Lighthouse Museum, Ian McNab and I climbed the steps of Kinnaird Head lighthouse to look at the light at close quarters. Once set in motion, the three ton light could be moved by the pressure of a finger. I quoted from my poem 'Castle Turned Lighthouse' (*Collected Poems*) written in 1943, 'ballbearing frictionless lamp'. Ian McNab pointed out they were not ballbearings. They were 'tapered rollers'. This set the poem going. I had met the whole man, engineer, singer, Brocher.

Invocation (p. 214)

21.	The occasion was the annual party of the Scottish Poetry Library. The Director, Tessa Ransford, had published *Medusa*, a collection of her poems. The library contains the works of poets past and present. Not far from the library in the High Street had been Sibbald's Library and, following it, Ramsay's Library.

Epistle 1: To Edwin Morgan (p. 215)

22. Edwin Morgan and Carl MacDougall invited me to contribute a poem to *New Writing, Scotland*. I had just returned from the United States, where at St Andrews College, North Carolina, I met Ezra Pound's daughter, Mary de Rachewiltz. She was curator of his manuscripts at Yale. She was annotating *The Cantos*. She thanked me for the information about Joseph MacLeod. I told her how he persuaded Elliot to publish MacLeod's first collection of poems, *The Ecliptic*, in 1928. To bring to mind something of the Pound 'atmosphere' I allowed into my letter 'cd' for could and 'sd' for should.

Epistle 5: A Thank-You to John Bellany (p. 219)

23. The three figures of fisherman have a religious implication. In his Introduction to the Catalogue for the 1986 exhibition of paintings, watercolours and drawings at the Scottish National Gallery of Modern Art, Keith Hartley wrote: 'But Bellany held tight to his convictions and was not afraid to tackle even the most traditional of subjects – the Crucifixion.'

    Yet the subject matter is far removed from the accepted iconography of classical paintings. 'In Allegory (1964) he established a basic approach to the raw material of his own experiences . . . The three gutted fish, nailed up to dry on their posts . . . are an allegory of the Crucifixion, and of all the cruelty, suffering and sacrifice that that event symbolised.' This is as Keith Hartley described, part of a 'monumental scheme'. The three fishermen, shabby, cast down, but with grim determination in their features is realistic yet evidently reveals that religious interpretation of life accepted by those who hunt fish.

At Mayakovsky's Statue (p. 221)

24. Mayakovsky, an idealist communist, turned against the Soviet bureaucracy. Frustrated, he committed suicide. I visited the statue, which was bronze, not stone; but the stone suited my purpose.

The Crescent (p. 223)

25. Number 33, the end house. Martin Prestige was married to Lucina.

Elizabeth in the Garden (p. 224)

26. The windflower plant was given to my wife by William Gillies (the painter) from his garden at Temple village, East Lothian, in the late 1960s. Apparently by the 1980s I had forgotten its name. I attempted and failed to write the poem, apart from the first lines, mislaid them and found them about 1995, the year after my wife's death.

Weys of Self-Preservin Natur (p. 227)

27. *Sweet Thames* Edmund Spenser.
28. *The City of London* William Dunbar.
29. *The New Testament in Scots* W.L. Lorimer (1983).

The Chair (p. 230)

30. The drawing was for the cover of *Interim* (University of Nevada Press) by Lucinda Wilder Stevens. Quotations used and adapted from Van Gogh's letters to his brother Theo.

Pursuit (p. 233)

31. The quotations in the poem make reference to *Paul Cézanne: Correspondence*, recueillié et préfacée par John Rewald, Paris, Bernard Grasset, 1978.
32. By 'house of being' Rilke meant words.

Velazquez (p. 240)

33. The references are to two paintings, *An Old Woman Cooking Eggs*, and *Water-seller of Seville*.

2000 (p. 251)

34. In the poem there is also the line, 'We see the brightness of a new page', which I have adapted. The poem is from Rilke's *Book of Hours: Love Poems to God* (1898). The translation of the book is by Anita Barrows and Joanna Macy (New York: Riverhead Books).

Lucina – To the Lighthouse! (p. 254)

35. On 10 March 1999 Lucina Prestige, Bill Gait the former lighthouse keeper and I climbed to the level of the light of Kinnaird Lighthouse, Fraserburgh, and then outside on to the narrow platform running round the light, from which the outside of the glass could be cleaned. We completed the circuit. No new experience to me, but Lucina being an initiate – and the date being my ninetieth birthday – heightened the sensation of the place and its environment. We were in Fraserburgh for the launch of my book *Pursuit*. So I came to write the above lines for Lucina.

Returning to the Broch (p. 255)

36. The Broch, local name for Fraserburgh.
37. Partans – edible crabs.
38. Greenbacks – small crab when as safticks they had lost their shells and were used for bait.
39. Cumpers – a fish with a big head and spikes on it.
40. Flukes – small flounders.
41. The iron hoops, heated by the fires, having expanded as they were hammered, contracted as they cooled, and made the barrels water-tight.
42. 'I am an atheist', declared to my father, who asked for his reasons. These having been given, my father said: 'I can give you better reasons for that,' and proceeded to do so.

The Eye – In Memoriam Tadeusz Kantor (p. 258)

43. Tadeusz Kantor, painter and sculptor, and also an innovator in experimental theatre, developed his central concept from the play *The Water Hen* by Stanislaw Witkiewicz. From this 'I created the idea of what I call "scenic pre-existence".' (Kantor). The play was presented by Kantor during the Edinburgh International Festival of 1972 in 'the Poor House', which may have been used as a storage for grain.
44. Duncan Ban Macintyre.
45. The *Interruption* affects performers and audience, both being of the same universe, under surveillance of Closed Circuit TV. When an event happens, to which the rules and rituals of the society cannot respond, its heart stops. It can be reanimated only by one who lives outside society. There is no precedent for a murdered body on the table.
   A different surveyor, The Eye has taken the place of CCTV. Whoever looks at it, it follows. The Nightwatchman is neither of the audience nor performers. He finds a place for the body where it can become a fiction to which an appropriate response can be given, and society can be itself again. Tadeus Kantor plays a similar role in other plays.
46. The Eye, Genesis 4:8. *La conscience* by Victor Hugo.
47. 'no sound was heard'. In 1930 I visited James Howie, then a medical student, now Professor Sir James Howie, in his digs at Ferryhill Place, Aberdeen, because he had a gramophone record of the Lener Quartet playing the last quartets of Beethoven. Since then I have met people who have not been in heaven after hearing them.

The Singing of the Foxes (p. 266)

48. In 2000 Mozambique was disastrously flooded.

City Inscape (p. 274)

49. Alexander III
50. Deacon Brodie, respectable citizen by day, thief by night, thought he would escape the gallows by the insertion of a device which would diminish the effect of the noose on his neck. He was wrong.
51. The Museum of Scotland.

Waiting Room – Leuchars December (p. 278)

52. Edwin Muir's 'war-time' job was at the Food Office. It lasted until 1942, when he was appointed to the British Council in Edinburgh. Leuchars, Fife, was the location of his visionary poem 'The Wayside Station' from which he made his daily return journey; his home was St Andrews. The number of 'war-planes' have recently been increased.

The Song of Henry Cockburn (p. 280)

53. 'The Song of Henry Cockburn' can justifiably carry this title on account of every descriptive term in it being taken from Cockburn's *Memorials of his Time* and *The Journal*. For the sake of rhythm and form, I have condensed and rearranged some of the precedents for this plagiarism, the most notable being Shakespeare's use of North's translation of Plutarch's biography of Antony in his play *Antony and Cleopatra*. In his Introduction to the play (The Caxton *Shakespeare Vol. 18*) Sidney Lee wrote: 'at times, even in the heat of the tragedy, the speeches of the hero and the heroine are transferred bodily from North's prose'.

Alphabetical List of Poems

Glossary

a	all	*carfuffle*	commotion
aa	everybody	*cauld*	cold
afore	before	*chiel*	fellow
a'body	everybody	*chievin*	achieving
aboot	about	*chine, chyne*	chain
agen	again	*claes*	clothes
ahint	behind	*clash*	talk, gossip
aifter	after	*close*	passageway (gen. to a
aince	once		tenement)
airches	arches	*codlin*	small cod
airn	iron	*connach'd*	finished
an lat thae	and allow those	*coorse*	rough
aneath	beneath	*coost*	cast
anither	another	*corrieneuchin*	conversing intimately
atween	between	*coup*	turn over
auld	old	*crood*	crowd
aye	always	*cud*	could
ayont	beyond	*dae*	do
ba game	ball game	*deaved*	deafened
bairn	child	*deef*	deaf
bairnie	little child	*deein*	dying
baith	both	*deid*	dead
ben maist	inmost	*derk*	dark
beryall	jewel, jewel like	*dirdit*	buffeted
bi	by	*dooncome*	downfall
bit	but	*doon-takin*	humiliation
bittock	a little bit	*doot*	doubt
blackie	black dog	*doun*	down
blaw	blow	*doups*	buttocks
bleat	stupid	*duin wioot*	done without
bleeze	blaze	*echts*	owns
blin	blind	*ee*	eye
blint	blinded	*een*	eyes
blootered	booted	*e'en*	even
bodie	body, human being	*eeseless*	useless
bondit	bonded	*eidently*	diligent
braid	broad	*elbuck*	elbow
braith	breath	*eneuch*	enough
brak	break	*ettled*	purposed
braw	fine	*fae, frae*	from
breist	breast	*faain*	falling
brig, brigge	bridge	*faither*	father
Broch	local name for	*Faithlie*	Fraserburgh
	Fraserburgh	*faur eence*	where once
Broch loon	Fraserburgh boy	*feart*	afraid
brocht	brought	*feenished*	finished
buik	book	*fit*	foot
cairry	carry	*fit,s deein?*	what's doing?
cam	came	*fit wye?*	what way

flasht	flashed
flim-flam-fleerie	flimsy, superficial
flooers	flowers
foo	full
foozlin	overcoming
fou's aa?	how's everybody?
fuff	puff of wind
full the boxes foo	fill the boxes full
gabs	chatters
gaed	went
gaithered	gathered
gan gyte	gone crazy
gang	go
gangrel	a wandering tramp or hobo
gawk	stare idly
gawpt	gaped
geck	stare
gied	given
gien	given
gin	if
girn	complain
gowden	golden
graip	an iron pronged fork
grander	a grand person
greetin	weeping
grippit	gripped
gryte	great
gryte hearted	great hearted
guid-wife	wife
gweed	good
hail	whole
hame	home
hantle	a fair number
haud	hold
hauden	holding, huddling
haun	hand
heich	high
heid	head
heid o't	head of it
heilan deems	highland women
heilster gowdie	head over heels
heist	hoist
hert	heart
hertit	hearted
hid	had
hid the died *chack knockit*	had the death watch beetle knocked
hine awa	far away
his	us
his loons	us boys
hisna	has not
hist	hurry
hoo	how
ile an saut	oil and salt
ill teenit	ill tempered
ingans	onions
ingaun	ingoing
ither	other
ithers	others
jile	jail
jined	joined
jinkit	dodged
jist	just
keek	look, peep
ken	know
kenna	know not
kenspeckle	show-off, conspicuous
kent	knew
kindlin	kindling wood
kitchie	kitchen
kittled	tickled
lang	long
lang syne	long ago
lealty	loyalty
leeds	languages
licht	light
lichtly	lightly
lichtnin	lightening
lift clood yokit	a sky with clouds linked together
look awa	look away
loup	leap
loupin	leaping
lowe	glow
ludgins	lodgings
lugs	ears
lumpen	souless mass
ma	my
maik	halfpenny
mair	more
maist	most
mannie	man
mart	market
maun	must
meat	food
meen	moon
mell	melee
mell't	mingled
merchantis	merchants
meth	might
mindin	remembering
mither	mother
mixter-maxter	mixed up
monkey	made a fool of
mou	mouth
mows	joke
mune	moon
neeps	turnips
never fecht your *meat man*	do not quarrel with your job
ony	only

oor	our	*saut*	salt
oot	out	*saxty*	sixty
oot-bye	outside, nearby	*scartit*	scratched
oot o' sicht	out of sight	*sclimman*	climbing
oot, stracht	straight ahead	*scrawled*	scrambled
orra loon	odd jobs boy	*scutter*	play about
owre	over	*sel*	self
partan	edible crab	*sgriobh*	write (Gael.)
pechin	breathing heavily	*shall*	shell
peep	low light	*sheenan*	shining
peelie-wally	sickly, feeble	*shaucle*	a huddle
peerie	small	*shuin*	shoes
Peterheid	Peterhead	*shavie*	deceitful
peyed	payed	*shift*	move about
pints	points	*shot*	catch (catch of fish)
pit it	put it	*sic*	such
pit-mirk	pitch-dark	*sic a girnan*	such a complaining
pit-oot	put out	*sicht*	sight
pitten	putting	*siller*	silver
plooed	ploughed	*skirl*	scream
pooch	pouch	*skeely*	skilful
pooer	power	*skraiches*	screeches
pot in the		*slipt, slippit*	slipped
wrinkled sand	a deep hole sometimes	*sma-boukit*	small built
	causing suction	*sma glen*	small valley
preen-heid	pin head	*sma' licht*	small light
puckle	few	*smert*	smart, be quick
Puddlestinker	a person who lived in	*smore a*	smother everything
	Hanover Street, Fraser	*snash*	insult, impudence
	burgh, known many years	*socht*	sought
	ago as Puddlestink, on	*sog*	soaked or wet place
	account of its slummy	*sonsy*	buxom
	appearance	*soom*	swim
puir	poor	*soon't*	sounded
pylers	pillars	*sooth*	south
quaet	quiet	*sough*	sudden intake of breath
quines	lasses, girls	*souk*	suck
raucle	rough	*soun*	sound
rax	reach	*spelding*	dried fish
raxed	reached	*spelding frae*	
reeshle	rustle	*the rack*	dried fish taken from the
retour	return		rack on which they were
richt	right		hung
rin-in	run in	*spewed*	vomited
risin	rising	*sproot*	sprout
ryvers	rivers	*squeel*	school
sae	so	*stane*	stone
saft	soft	*stap*	stop
safticks	greenback crabs used	*strang*	strong
	for bait	*staun*	stand
sair	sore	*steamy*	wash-house
sair tyave	sore (hard) labour	*steen*	stone
sangs	songs	*steen wa*	stone wall
sanle	sand eels	*stookies*	stucco
saps	bread soaked in milk,	*stracht*	straight
	children's food	*stramash*	commotion
sarks	shirts	*strang souch*	strong breathing

stravaig	wander	*wioot*	without
swack	flexible, supple	*wir*	ours
swall	swell	*wis*	we
swalt	swollen	*wites*	waits
swanne	swan	*witin*	waiting
sweir	unwilling	*wrack*	seaweed
s'wester	sou'wester, waterproof hat	*wrang wey*	wrong way
		wuids	woods
swymme	swim	*wun*	wind
syne	then	*wurd*	word
tae	to	*wyngis*	wings
tak tent	give heed	*wyte*	wait
taigelt	tangled	*yammer*	talk volubly, talkative
tap	top	*yelloch*	yell, scream
tatties	potatoes	*yestreen*	yesterday
tee the gruns	close to the fishing grounds	*yird, yirth*	earth
teemed	emptied		
teen	temper (v.), taken (n.)		
teuchats	lapwing		
thegither	together		
thochts	thoughts		
thon	yon, that		
thrawn	obstinate		
threided	threaded		
thunner	thunder		
tatties	potatoes		
ticht	tight		
till	until		
til' a' richt	into it all right		
tither	the other		
toun	town		
trimmlin	trembling		
tuim	empty		
twa	two		
tyave	hard labour		
unkennan	unknowing		
unnerstan	understand		
vennels	narrow lane between houses		
virr	vigour		
vrocht	worked hard		
wa	wall		
wanchancy	treacherous		
warlds	worlds		
Warld's End	Edinburgh vennel		
wark	work		
watter	water		
wecht	weight		
weel	well		
weemen	women		
weys	ways		
wha	who		
wha's	who is this?		
whaur	where		
whins	gorse		
wi freens	with friends